Startup Idea
Action Plan

Written By
Ryan Mulvihill

Startup Idea Action Plan

Validate the Startup and Get Customers in 7 Days, When All You Have is a Business Idea

By Ryan Mulvihill

Dedication

To the thrills of entrepreneurship, and the many friends and family who have supported me along the way. I could not be living the way I am without your constant support.

Disclaimer and Legalese

This ebook contains information about subject matters associated with starting a business and calling potential customers. This information is not legal advice and should not be treated as such. Ryan Mulvihill is not an attorney and does not offer legal advice (no matter how much I know you want it from me). If you have any questions about a legal matter you should talk to a lawyer.

I have made every attempt to make sure the information in this book is accurate, but it is impossible to guarantee 100% accuracy. It is also impossible to guarantee any particular result or outcome from your business endeavours. I can only give you what worked for my clients and I, so results may vary. Laws and software tools change and this ebook cannot represent all of these changes.

Copyright © 2015 by Ryan Mulvihill

All rights reserved

Your Free Bonus

I want to make pursuing your business idea easier for you.

I have created a short guide to jumpstart your entrepreneurial ventures—with 8 different tools to teach you how to become organized and productive while turning your startup into a thriving business.

"8 Secret Tools for Bootstrapping your Startup Idea to Success"

Get the PDF at growanempire.com/resources

I'll give you a hint, these tools aren't "Evernote" or "DropBox" These are the lesser known tools that create the biggest changes when it comes starting your own business.

You are pretty much guaranteed to find an essential startup tool that you didn't even know existed.

Along with this PDF you can get the templates mentioned in this book:
- *The easy guide to getting 100s of lead in your market for less than $50*
- *The Complete Cold Call Battle Plan template*
- *Your First 20 Calls Workbook*

Again you can find all there resources at:
growanempire.com/resources

Table of Contents

Chapter One - Start Up Smart — 1
    First Step to Start Up — 3
    Who You Gonna Call? — 7
    The Money's in the List — 10
    Make Your Leads Feel the Heat — 19

Chapter Two - Telephobia — 25
    What Scares You? — 27
    Awkwardness Happens Often — 30
    Scary Story Time — 34
    Rejected! — 42

Chapter Three - Life's a Pitch — 49
    Basic Pitches — 51
    Short and Sweet — 56
    Elevator Conversation — 59
    Counter Attack! — 63
    Make Your Pitch Deck — 68

Chapter Four - The Hierarchy — 73
    What Do You Want? — 75
    You Never Get If You Never Ask — 83
    What Do I Want to Learn? — 89
    When Do I Ask? — 92
    Scaring Secretaries — 101
    Objections, Your Honor! — 104
    Your Cold Call Battle Plan — 111

Chapter Five - Doing the Calls — 119

    The Grasshopper Is Ready — 121
    Fun With Roleplay — 127
    Cold Call Time — 131
    The Pep Talk You Need — 134
Chapter Six - After Your Calls — 137
    You Did It! — 139
    Track Your Calls — 149
    Taking Action on Your Info — 153
    Building your Case — 156
    What If My Idea Fails? — 159
    Pre-Selling — 162
    This Is Where I Leave You — 167
Chapter X - The End — 169
    Acknowledgements — 171

STARTUP IDEA ACTION PLAN

Chapter One:
Start Up Smart

Ryan Mulvihill

First Step to Start Up

YOU HAVE AN idea for a business! Great! Now what? Do you brainstorm ideas for a name? Do you hire a software developer to start building the product? Do you start pitching your idea to venture capitalists to get funding?

When you come up with a business idea, the first question you have to answer is "Do people want to buy what I am looking to sell?" All other points are secondary. There's no point brainstorming pun-tastic names or spending money on a nice website if you can't answer that primary question.

This is what I am going to teach you in this book: an easy-to-follow process that will show you how to reach out to your market and find out if people will buy your product. It's cheap, easy to set up, and will teach you skills you need to make your business idea successful. Get ready to learn the Startup Action Plan.

Through this process you will answer the questions that are most important in determining whether your business idea will be a success or a flop.

- You will find out if people actually want to pay for what you want to sell.
- You will get a list of interested customers together to sell to

when it launches.
- You will find out exactly what pains your market is looking to solve.
- You will get referrals and introductions to more people in your market to sell to.
- You will learn how to effectively sell to your target market.
- You will never again be stuck wondering, "Is my business idea worth pursuing?"
- You will end up with a list of customers who are interested in buying your product

So what is this process? I'll explain it in two ways:

The Keep It Simple Stupid (KISS) Explanation

You have an idea that could make some people's lives or businesses better. You think that they are really going to like it, so you decide to reach out to a bunch of possible customers to see if they think it is an awesome idea too. You gather a list of people who may like your idea, emailing and calling them to explain your idea. They give you feedback on your idea and it starts to evolve into an even better idea. After talking to 20–30 people, you start to know how much these people will pay, what features they need, how to properly sell to them, and a hundred other tidbits of information that make your business idea very doable. You start to feel confident in your business idea, and now you feel comfortable investing your time and money into turning this idea into a reality.

The Business Savvy Explanation

It is a process for gathering a contact list together, beating your fears and limiting beliefs regarding talking to your market, developing a plan on how to communicate with your market, and learning whether your idea is a winner or a loser. You'll be using an aggressive process of cold calling and cold emailing to reach out to your potential customers. There is no need to spend months building a blog and hoping they come to you—you are going to reach out to them first.

A quick note about cold calling. Most people are put off by the term "cold calling," and I don't blame them. COLD CALLING IS DEAD, blog articles will exclaim. The C word brings up the idea of one of those cruise companies calling thousands of random people hoping they find one who really does believe they won a free cruise. That is NOT what you are doing. You are just reaching out to the businesspeople that could benefit from your business idea. Some people will be interested, some will not, but no one will label you an aggressive, annoying phone salesperson. Cold calling isn't bad or wrong—some people have just abused it. I'm going to teach you how to be an honorable, charming cold caller that people will be happy to talk to. Glad I could clear that up for you.

This task may seem daunting, but don't worry—I'll walk you through this entire process, step by step to make you a cold call warrior. It's not nearly as hard as you think. I will lay out this process very clearly to get you inspired to take action.

All you need to start this process off is a business idea. You could be literally be starting from a vague business idea and turn it into a defined product with a bunch of customers eager to buy—in the span of a week!

On the other hand, the research you gather indicate that people don't want to buy your business idea. This is also a good scenario for you, as you will know that this wasn't the right business to start before you have invested your time and energy into it. That faster you learn the business was doomed from the start, the faster you can start researching your next awesome idea.

Indeed, when you learn this process, it is a lot like having a superpower. You will know a flexible process to contact a market for the first time, and learn what you need to know about starting a business in that industry. It removes the question of "Will they buy this thing?" because you have the knowledge of how to contact them and find out. You will have the power to create business from scratch whilst gathering potential customers — whereas before you would have been stuck thinking "How do I start this business?"

After learning the Startup Action Plan you will be transformed from a dreamy wantrepreneur living in fantasy land to a hustling action taker, turning ideas into reality. You will be learning how to cold call into a market and effectively attack any business idea. I need a punchier name for this process. The Startup Action Plan will henceforth be called Cold Call Karate. Because if you are going to wage the war that is starting a business, you are going to have to know how to fight.

Who You Gonna Call?

IN ORDER TO get this Cold Call Karate process started, you have to have a good idea of who your potential customers are. You need to get as precise as possible with exactly WHO you want to be contacting. The more precise your profile of your ideal customer, the better your results will be. Here are a few examples:

- If you want to sell your custom-branded umbrellas to fashion boutiques, then you would want to talk to the manager of a boutique. You would also probably want to contact independent boutiques, as they would have an easier time bringing unique products into the store.
- If you have a product you want to sell to hotels then your customer isn't a "hotel"—your customer would be the purchasing manager of a hotel.
- If you have a software idea to help chiropractors manage their businesses, then you would want to talk to the office manager or head chiropractor.
- If you have an idea for using quad copters to do aerial mapping for landscapers, you would want to talk to the project managers in a landscaping company.

Exercise 1.1

As in the above examples, figure out the exact profile of the people you want to contact. If you have a couple different types of customers you want to contact, that is fine as well. Fill out the following information for each type of customer you want to target. (Again, if you are only targeting one type of customer, that's alright too)

Position – Niche – Location – Independent (yes, no or either)

Depending on what sort of product you are launching, it may be better to target independent stores that aren't part of a larger chain. You would do this because independent stores can make decisions about bringing on new products more easily than chain stores. Sometimes it won't matter—just make your best guess about whether a company being independent or part of a larger chain will make a difference to you.

Same goes for location. Sometimes it will matter where these businesses are located, sometimes it will not. It's up to you to decide what will matter for your business idea.

Here are some examples of customer targets

Hiring manager – Real estate companies – In Toronto – Either

Head chiropractor – Chiropractic clinics – North America – Independent

Boss – SEO service business – Located anywhere – Independent

———————

After you have figured out who you want to target, you can get your list created. The more specific your idea of who you want to contact, the easier time you will have with the Cold Call Karate process.

THE MONEY'S IN THE LIST

NOW YOU HAVE a pretty good idea of who you want to call, or at least what business niche you are going after. But how are you going to get their contact information? Uncle Ted, your real estate agent uncle, can only put you in touch with a couple other real estate agents. After that you are going to be stuck flipping through the phone book for new leads, right?

Wrong.
There is a way to get hundreds of leads in your market with only an hour of work, for less than $50. That way is by using a virtual assistant to do the work searching for you. In this section I'll be taking you through how to choose and hire a VA (i.e., someone who is willing to do work for you, at a low cost, and over the Internet).

I'm teaching you a new technique for contacting your market, so why would I give you technical information on how to hire a VA? My advice would be useless if you didn't put it into action. In order to contact your market, you need to have your market's contact information. This is your leads list. Getting a leads list completed may take a few days, so I want to help you get it started ASAP.

Depending on the niche you contact, it may take some time to get a leads list together (or have someone do it for you). I don't want you to start learning how to call, only to get scared about actually doing the calls and procrastinate on getting a leads list together to never do any calling. I've trained enough people to know what excuses you are going to make, so I'm going to do my best to get you to actually take action.

Getting your list together will also give you more skin in the game, so to speak. You will have already invested in getting this work started, so it will be harder for you to drop when you feel a few tinges of fear.

On the flip side, if you already have a current customer or prospects list together, then feel free to skim this section. I just want to make sure that, when you are prepared to make the calls, you don't have to wait for a VA to put a list together.

This will take you an hour to set up, and will greatly benefit your progress the sooner you do it. Even a list of just 100 prospects is enough to begin your Cold Call Karate experiments.

Consider this a small investment in pursuing your business idea. If throwing down a few dollars to research your market and find potential customers is too high of an investment for you, then you probably won't be taking any action on your idea. You might as well throw in the towel now.

But I don't want you to do that. I want you to give this process a try. Even if your business idea turns out to be a dud, what you learn from contacting your market will be immensely helpful for your next venture. Don't think of this process as a win or lose situation, think of it as win or learn. Whether you find that people are interested in your product or that they have no need for it, you will come out way ahead when you use this approach.

Now that we're all on board, it is time to get down to creating your first leads list. How do you hire someone to create a list of potential customers for you? It's easier and cheaper than you think...

By using a virtual assistant you can have hundreds of leads in any B2B market in three days, for less than 50$ and an hour of work on your part.

My students and I have been very successful in getting a virtual assistant to create a list of leads to call. Some people have told that me they want to create their leads lists themselves, and I have to say, that is the biggest waste of time I can think of! It would take multiple hours, and be frustratingly boring.

Using a virtual assistant from Upwork is easy and affordable. It is the smart way to get leads in your target market for you to call later. Here are all the steps you need in order to get someone to build a leads list for you.

———————

Exercise 1.2

Follow these steps to get your leads list created. It is vital for the Cold Call Karate process to work, so don't hesitate in getting your leads list done. The template for this Upwork job posting is available on my site growanempire.com/resources to make this process easy for you.

Step 1: Create a profile on Upwork

Go to www.upwork.com. Nothing fancy, just upload a credit card and information so you can hire a VA. This is the biggest and most trusted site out there when it comes to using virtual assistants, so you can rest easy putting your credit card details on it.

Step 2: Create a job posting

Startup Idea Action Plan

The act of searching the Web for contact information is called "Web scraping." In order to find a freelancer capable of creating a quality list for you, you need to attract applications with a job posting. Here is a sample job posting for the veterinarian market, which you can tweak as necessary for your particular market. Again, this template is available at growanempire.com/resources for you to download, so you don't have to re-type everything. When looking at this template, imagine swapping out any vet-related information for your market's info:

Start of template:

Category: Admin Support - Web Research

Job Name: Web Scraping for Veterinarian's Contact Info with Clear Instructions

Summary:

I need someone to compile a leads list of veterinarians who are currently working in clinics.

The leads need to fit these specifications:

I want 300 leads from Ontario, Canada.

I want 300 leads from anywhere else in Canada.

I want 300 leads from anywhere else in English speaking countries.

In total, I need 900 leads.

I only want one veterinarian from each clinic—I do not want multiple veterinarians that work at the same clinic.

I require the personal emails of each veterinarian. No emails that like "info@clinic.com," "staff@clinic.com," or "clinic@gmail.com," or anything of that sort. Use your best judgment for this and get personal-sounding emails like john.smith@clinic.com.

Finding personal emails is the hard part. When scraping the Web, look for the personal email information first, and then look for all the other information associated with that veterinarian's email.

I require the following information from each veterinarian to be organized into an Excel sheet: name, email, phone number (this can be the clinic's phone number), clinic name, clinic location (for the Ontario clinics I need the exact address, for all the other clinics I just need the country they are in, like Canada, America, UK, Singapore or Australia), and clinic website.

I am looking for a fixed price for a leads list of this magnitude. Please reply with your bid for the job. Bids of over $70 will be ignored. Lowest bid or best sales pitch gets the job.

*If you have read this whole job posting tell me what your favourite colour is in your answer to the screening question.

Skills: Data Entry, Microsoft excel, Web scraping

How would you like to pay: Fixed price

Entry Level: Intermediate

Budget: $50 (depends on the amount of leads you are going for)

Marketplace exposure: Maximum

Number of hires: One freelancer

Qualifications: Minimum score of at least 4.5

No cover letter needed

Screening question: What do you do to keep conversations interesting?

End of template

Feel free to use this template when posting your job. If there are some extra things you want your VA to put into your Excel spreadsheet, then add it into your job posting. Just make sure you keep your instructions as simple as possible.

Step 3: Set your price

Set a fixed price for the job, NOT HOURLY. Budget $10 to $20 for every 100 leads for a general market, like veterinarians. So if you are trying to get 400 leads, set the price at $50 or so. Freelancers will then bid on it. If you are targeting a very specific markct where leads are hard to find, you may have to budget more for this. Same goes for trying to find the contact information for higher-ups in a business.

Finding the contact information for a general manager of a hotel is more difficult then finding the general phone numbers of plumbing companies. Do a quick Google search looking for your target market's contact information. See how long it takes you to find a few names, phone numbers and emails to judge how easy it is to find this info.

Step 4: Post your job

If you made the posting easy to follow and set a good price, then in about 24 hours you should have roughly 20 decent freelancers bidding on your job.

Step 5: Select your freelancer

Message your favorite freelancers, who will bid on your job and confirm that they can complete the job to your specifications.

The best way to quickly screen freelancers is to message then and ask them a question about the specifics of the job. Ask something like:

"Hey, thanks for the reply. I just want to make sure you are up to this task. Can you show me an example of other Web scraping work you've done in the past?"

Their answer will tell you volumes about their English levels and what type of work you can expect from them.

After your little screening question, award the best freelancer your job. Since this is such a small, simple task, there is no need to phone interview them or anything.

Choose someone with good English skills, close to a 5-star reputation, and over 50 ratings. With those qualifications you can be pretty sure they will do a good job. You want to pick an experienced freelancer, as inexperienced ones will be a huge headache. Be careful, as inexperienced freelancers will promise you the world and fail to deliver. Read their profiles and see if they specifically mention being good at Web scraping. Then just follow your gut. If a freelancer is highly rated, they had to have worked hard for that rating.

Expect three to seven days to be the time it will take to build a leads list for you. Applicants will include this time estimate in their proposals.

If you want to use a freelancer I was very satisfied with, then check out Raju Kakoti from Info-Rich on Upwork. This is also a good example of the type of freelancer you want to hire. If you use them, tell them that RyanMulvi sent you.

Step 6: Enjoy the leads list

If the freelancer did fine, release their escrow funds and give them a good rating. If the freelancer did a bad job, then freeze their escrow payment until they complete the work to your satisfaction. I usually give a freelancer a smaller job, like 200 to 300 leads for their first job. That way, if they do a crappy job, I haven't lost very much.

As for what constitutes a bad list, things like duplicate entries, contacts that are outside your target market, and general sloppiness usually mean a freelancer won't be getting a second hire from me.

— — — — — — — — —

Extra tips on using freelancers:
- Make your instructions as idiot proof as possible. Not to say that freelancers are idiots—they just may not understand your cunning linguistics.
- Make your deliverables SMART: Specific, Measurable, Attainable, Relevant, Timely
- Don't be afraid to ask them to fix their work if you're not happy with it—you are the boss, after all.
- Read the *The 4-Hour Work Week* (expanded edition) page 121 and onwards on great instructions for using virtual assistants. It's in the older version too, just a different page. This book has a ton of relevant information about outsourcing, so check it out here if you haven't already
- If this is your first time hiring freelancers and you are interested in having them do other types of work for you, I recommend reading *Virtual Freedom* by Chris Ducker to learn about hiring teams of freelancers—but only if you want to start using freelancers for more

complicated tasks in your business.

- Make sure you specify that you want PERSONAL emails, otherwise your VA will give you a list of useless info@clinic.com emails, but it will be YOUR FAULT.

Conclusion

Using a freelancer from Upwork is the best, fastest, and cheapest way to create a list of leads to call through in order to validate your business idea. Get this job posting up as soon as possible so you can take action as soon as possible. Go to www.upwork.com and get your profile set up. The sooner you get this list, the sooner you can start talking to your customers!

Make Your Leads Feel the Heat

WHEN YOU FINALLY get your leads list, you should talk to them before you talk to them. What I mean by this is that you should send them an email first to open them up to the idea of talking to you. I call it sending a "Preheater" email.

After you have gathered your list you will be sending out an email to your contact list to tell them a little about yourself, and to hopefully heat a few of those cold leads into warm leads. Hence the email "Preheater" strategy.

Once you have your contact list together you can upload it to an online service like MailChimp will allow you to mass email your list and insert merge tags, making it simple to customize your email. You could send them out yourself, but that would take a long time. MailChimp will just allow you to send out a mass of emails and track how many people opened, how many times they opened, and how many replied. Go to MailChimp.com if you want to check it out for yourself. I prefer MailChimp as it is very easy to use and figure out, and convenient for the Cold Call Karate method.

The email you send should be something simple—only a few sentences long, with just enough information to whet your contact's appetite and encourage them to correspond with you.

Here are a few examples:

Specific Problem Email

Subject: Strange Question

"Hey (Name),

I'm (My Name) and I'm doing research into the dentistry market in order to help you reduce client slippage. I was wondering if you are currently taking any measures to reduce the amount of patients that fall through the cracks."

Feedback Email

Subject: What do you think?

Hey (Name),

I have been doing research into a new type of promotional item for independent fashion boutiques. It is a folding purse hook that can be branded to your boutique's preference. I'd love to talk to you and get your feedback on the idea, to see if it's something you could actually use.

Challenges Email

Subject: Challenges Vets Face

"Hi, I'm Ryan and I'm doing research into the business challenges veterinarians face on a regular basis, with the hopes of developing a software to help out with them. I was wondering if I could have a quick chat with you to learn about your market."

The Famous 9 Word Email (AKA one-sentence email)

Subject: Quick Question

"Hey (name), are you finding your current CRM sucks?"

Feel free to make up your own email. Keep it super short so your prospect actually reads it—four sentences or less is perfect. Many people try to write their entire life's story into these preheater emails, only to find no one wants to read it, let alone respond.

Keep the subject lines vague so as to build intrigue with your prospect. I have found that more mysterious email subject lines get more opens. Get creative and try out a few different subject lines.

What you say in the email isn't too important, as long as it tries to prompt a reply from your target. If you send over 100 emails, you should at least get a few responses. If these targets are receptive, they will be the first people in your market you will be talking to. This will make your first couple of calls easier, as they are warm.

A side note here is that some people are afraid of spamming people and breaking laws in that regard. Firstly, researching a business idea and talking to your market is not "spamming." If anything, it is providing value. Spammers send out massive amounts of emails saying "BUY NOW." Entrepreneurs engage with their market.

Legally you are in the clear as well. There's this law called the CAN-SPAM act here in Canada that is aimed at trying reduce email spam. Technically it is legal to send emails to businesses. Business-to-business cold emailing is fine. If you bought a huge list of homeowners' emails off the Internet and sent 10,000 emails regarding a fantastic timeshare opportunity, then you would be breaking the law.

Another area people are worried about is getting people to "opt-in" before you can email them. Technically speaking MailChimp says you have to get people to opt-in before you can email them. Ignore this. MailChimp is worried that you have a huge list of people that you are spamming. Using their system to send a couple hundred emails is barely a blip on their radar, so email away. The worst that will happen is that they will stop your email campaign if many of your prospects label it as spam. When you actually want to launch a newsletter, then you can worry about getting opt-ins. For now we need to focus on the fastest and most efficient way of contacting your market, which is using their system to help send out a bunch of emails.

If you don't want to use MailChimp to send your emails then you can check out Streak. Which allows you to send email campaigns right from your inbox.

Now that I have put your fears, to rest you can start to think about the response you will get from the emails. A majority of the people you email will NOT respond to you. Don't lose sleep over the lack of response, as it is normal to have a low response rate.

Even though most people don't respond, you now have an "in" when you are calling them. When you speak to the secretary, you can say that you are following up on an email you sent to Mr. Blank. Even if Mr. Blank never looked at your email, it will make it much easier to talk to him. We will get into the call scripts soon, but for now just focus on getting those emails out ASAP.

—————————

Exercise 1.3

Create your version of the four different types of pitches listed above. It doesn't have to be the PERFECT pitch, just good enough that it could work for your market.

Choose your favourite one. Depending on your market, some pitch types may sound better depending on your business idea. Get a MailChimp campaign ready to go so you can send out this email to your leads list ASAP. MailChimp is free, and is very easy to get set up to send these out. Don't use a fancy template or pictures, just a simple text email.

Send out these emails as soon as your leads list is done. It may take a few days before you get your initial responses. This will give you a head start in creating your cold calling process.

Get those emails sent!

— — — — — — — — — —

Sending out these emails will help you get some skin in the game. When you start feeling like you should quit, you can think back to those couple of warm responses you got and push yourself forward to calling into your market. This is a process of pushing past your fears in starting a business, which is usually a scary process.

As for calling, you probably have quite a few fears when it comes to that. We should deal with those before we start the process.

Chapter Two:
Telephobia

Ryan Mulvihill

What Scares You?

WHAT ARE YOU afraid of? Are you some kind of wuss or something?

When people are initiating a process like this, they usually have some fears about talking to strangers. Your mom always told you not to, but you're old enough now to not heed her advice. I talk to strangers all the time and it has led to many awesome experiences and opportunities. You, however, are new to this, so you will naturally have some fears and avoidance when it comes to reaching out to your market.

You probably have some pretty legitimate fears when it comes to cold calling. Everyone does, so we're going to play a little game called "Write It Down."

Exercise 2.1

The rules of "Write It Down" are simple: I want you to brainstorm and think of every worst-case scenario that can happen when it comes to your calls. Make a list of every deep dark fear you have crawling around in that brain of yours, and define it as clearly as possible.

Don't hold back. If you're afraid of lightning striking, traveling through your phone line, and turning your brain into meatloaf, write it down in your list. (I hope you aren't afraid of the lightning thing, because that happens pretty infrequently.)

To help facilitate figuring out your list of fears think of these questions:

- What am I afraid of happening?
- What could go wrong?
- What would stop me from picking up the phone?

Many people write down things like:

I'm afraid that people will be angry I'm disturbing them and yell at me on the phone.

I'm afraid I'll forget what to say and make a complete fool of myself. Then they'll tell all their colleagues what a fool I am.

I'm afraid everyone will tell me my idea is terrible, and I will think I'm a failure at life.

These are a few to get you started. So don't hold back, write 'em all down!

Make your list right now, before reading any farther...

— — — — — — — — — —

After writing a list of your fears, take a look at this. Your fears probably fall into one of these categories:

Awkwardness

Angering someone

Scarcity/perfectionism

Rejection

Your idea failing

Gather 'round, boys and girls, and let me tell you a few little stories about these fears. Some of them will make you cringe, some will make you laugh, but all of them will teach you that your phone call-related fear is not something to be fearful of.

AWKWARDNESS HAPPENS OFTEN

MANY PROMINENT FEARS are going to be associated with awkwardness —specifically you being awkward on the phone. Things are not going to go your way a lot of the time. Things can get a little awkward sometimes Here are a few of my awkward experiences with cold calling...

Dealing with Death
"Miss Kilpatrick has passed away, I'm her husband, said the gruff man on the other end of the phone. What is the sales protocol for trying to sell a window cleaning to someone, only to find out they are dead? I certainly wasn't warned of this possibility in my sales training. I was, however, told to make every lead count. So do I sell to the next of kin?

This was one of the rare instances where I decided to let the sale slide. "I'm really sorry to hear that," I replied meekly. I wanted out of this situation. "Yeah, the cancer was just too much for her... I'm her widowed husband. Is there anything I can help you with?" Now I was really at a loss. What was I supposed to say? That is just one of the more awkward phone experiences I ever had, but the cringe-fest is just getting started.

Due to the nature of phone sales, you have very little control over what is going on. You can have grade-A scripts and prepare for every objection, and still end the call feeling like you got your teeth kicked in. These instances will make you tough. Facing your fears in cold calling is going to make you more powerful, like training in the mountains.

Accidental Harassment

"This is the third time you've called. WE ARE NOT INTERESTED! Why do you keep calling?" the lady on the other end of the phone yelled as she clicked the phone into the receiver. It's not that I wanted to call her multiple times, especially after the first conversation went badly. She just happened to have her number spread out a few times through my prospect list, and I hadn't noticed.

A clerical error from my virtual assistant was now an earful for me. That was a heap of awkwardness, trying to explain that I was not a salesman who didn't take no for an answer. It was simply an honest mistake that I called her a bunch of times, but she will never know that.

Accidental Misogyny

"I'm calling on behalf of Michelle, the little girl who gave you a window cleaning quote." I cringed as the words "little girl" slipped off my tongue into reality. But I decided to solider forward with the pitch, hoping my prospect wouldn't notice. "Why are you calling Michelle a <u>little girl</u>?" said the pissed off woman on the other end of the phone, clearly noticing. I had just said the most unintentionally sexist line of my life, and now had to face the consequences.

I call my co-worker Michelle "Little Lady" all the time because she's short, and a lady, and I think I'm a hilarious nicknamer. Somehow I'd not only revealed her nickname to a customer, but through a brain fart I'd botched it and replaced "lady" with "girl." I now epitomized sexism to Miss Boyer, all because of one clumsy sentence. I think I still tried to sell her some window cleaning work. She said no.

The point of these cringe-worthy tales is to show you that things will get awkward occasionally—just accept this reality. You will completely forget what you are saying mid-sentence. You will terribly mispronounce some prospect's names (if you call them the right name to begin with, of course). You will make an awkward joke once and a while. This especially happens to me, as I love to crack jokes with complete strangers over the phone. I consider myself quite punny. See, that right there was a terrible joke that could lead to an awkward silence. But it's not a big deal—just work past it when it happens.

Let's do a little test. What is the most awkward thing you remember someone doing in the last month? Odds are you can't remember anything specific, unless it was a really big deal. You have a crystal clear memory of every awkward experience that happened to you, but it is near impossible to remember the awkward things OTHER people have done. We have this sort of mental fallacy that we think everyone else can remember your awkward moments. They can't. All of those memories you have of your awkward moments are likely forgotten by everyone else.

The awkwardness you are going to experience during your phone calls is not going to be a big deal. It will be forgotten within 10 seconds of changing the subject. If it is as memorable as the tales I just regaled you with, then you will get a laugh out of it, eventually.

Accept that awkwardness will happen sometimes when you are pushing for what you want on the phone. Tim Ferriss wrote, "A man can be judged by the amount of uncomfortable conversations he is willing to make." Be willing to allow things to get uncomfortable on occasion, because you can handle it. Once you face a few awkward conversations, you will realize it's not such a big deal. You'll forget why you were even afraid in the first place.

Awkwardness is just the start of your fears, however...

Scary Story Time

BELOW ARE A few stories that will sound like some of the fears you'll face. Even though your fears are personal to you, they likely fit into one of these categories. I'm going to tell you about my experiences facing these fears, and philosophize about why you should ignore them.

Dealing with Angry People

Some people you talk to are just not very happy people—or, due to some miscommunication, they might label you as the devil. But very few people will actually get angry with you on the phone. It's only happened to me a handful of times. The story I'm about to tell you is about a certain lady who was probably convinced I was a weirdo who wanted to talk to her kids on the phone. (To be fair, her daughter sounded like the most mature eight-year-old I had ever talked to.)

It all started with me trying to prove a point in a crowded Starbucks. One of the members of my mastermind team was very afraid of cold calling potential customers to do research on her business idea. She was worried about people being angry with her and yelling at her on the phone, so I decided that I would step in to show her that people were generally nice on the phone.

"I'll bet you I can call up a random stranger and get a movie recommendation, without them being angry about me calling them," I claimed confidently. My entrepreneurial buddy thought otherwise. Eager to prove what a badass I was on the phone, I dialled a random local number and a girl picked up.

"Hello?"

"Hi, is this Carrie?"

"No, I think you have the wrong number."

"Oh, well that's OK. Hey, this is really random, but do you have any movie recommendations that I should watch tonight?"

"No, I don't."

"It's fine, any sort of suggestion would be great," I persisted. (Always pushing just a little harder is something I picked up from many years of cold calling.)

"STOP TALKING!" the lady on the other end screamed into the phone.

"Click." I hung up. That was one of my weirder calls, I thought to myself. I felt a tinge of guilt for a minute, but it was soon replaced with the hilarity of the lady's reaction on the phone.

Chris and I had a good laugh about it and didn't think much of the situation. But about half an hour later I received a call back from the same phone number, with a different crazed woman on the phone.

"How could you crank call an eight-year-old like that?" To be fair, she had sounded very mature for an 8 year old.

"Oh, sorry. I didn't know she was eight, and I was just doing a psychological study to see if strangers would give other strangers movie recommendations."

"How dare you do a study on my child, who do you think you are?"

Click, I hung up the phone, not wanting to deal with an overprotective mother's ranting.

She only called back three more times, leaving an angry voice mail calling me a creep and a bunch of other colorful words. She did not give me a movie recommendation. However she did recommend I never call her again. Sure, I felt a little guilty for a bit, but it quickly subsided into my most hilarious cold calling story to date.

On the rare occasion, you are going to talk to some very angry people during your calls. However, after you hang up, when the slightly guilty feeling wears off, you will have a hilarious story to share with your friends. In reality, these angry people will provide you with an entertaining story in the long run—and it will allow you to test out your newfound superpower.

What is this superpower, you ask?

Imagine if, the next time you were in a really difficult conversation, you had the ability to shut that person up with no consequences. They could be ranting and rambling, but with a wave of your hand you could make them disappear. If only life were so simple. I'll tell you a secret, though—when cold calling, you can do this.

This particular superpower is called hanging up the phone. While cold calling you may use this power as much as you like—so go wild!

When someone gets angry with you on the phone, you don't have to listen to any of their smack talk. You can cut them off cold and then laugh about them with your friends. Very few people will ever become angry with you on the phone, but when it does happen, it's hilarious. Maybe it won't be hilarious for a few minutes after the call is over, but trust me, you will see find the hilarity soon enough.

Wasting People's Time/Bothering People

You are going to hear this phrase a lot when you call:

"No, I'm not interested."

I've heard this phrase more times in a year than most people will in their entire lives. I was doing research into the chiropractic market, looking into the possibility of creating a software solution for their market, and wasn't getting many bites.

They were a busy market for sure, constantly running off to the next patient, but a few of them did have time to talk to me. Even when they had no interest in creating a software solution to help them out with their business, they would still tell me a little about their industry.

Odds are you won't be contacting heart surgeons midway through surgery. If someone is taking a phone call with you, they likely aren't in some life threatening situation where speaking to you for 30 seconds will affect their life in any way.

I never felt that I was asking for too much by reaching out to my target market, and, as far as I know, none of the people I spoke to felt it was a waste of time to talk to me. After all, I was reaching out to try and create some value for them, and try and solve problems they were facing in their industry. I felt I had a lot of value to offer the people I was speaking to, so therefore I never felt I was wasting people's time.

If you're reading this right now, odds are you are not selling something useless like timeshares in Florida. You believe that people will get value out of the conversation you are going to have with them on the phone. If they are not interested in speaking to you, then it's their loss. If they are not interested in your business idea, they probably still appreciate the call.

When you are offering value to people, you are never wasting their time or bothering them significantly. So do not worry—it's a non-issue. If they have time, they'll talk to you. If they don't, then it's no big deal.

Scarcity

Many people are afraid of running out of people to talk to, and that comes from their fear of scarcity. Strangely enough, I find this fear to be closely tied to perfectionism. People are afraid of having a limited number of people to sell to and call, so they think they have to make every call perfect. They never think they are ready to start calling because their pitch isn't perfected, of for a million other reasons.

"What if I run out of people to call?" They wonder aloud as they reach for the phone. "I better not call until I know everything about the person I'm talking to." So they spend an hour researching the person's past on LinkedIn, looking them up on Facebook, and finding every bit of obscure information on them person possible.

Then they make the call, only to hear the words, *"Sorry, Mr. X is away for the month on holiday. Think you could call back another time?"*

And just like that, all your time seems to have been wasted chasing the dragon you weren't ever going to catch.

First, I'll address the scarcity mindset. You will not ever run out of people to call—and if it is possible to run out, then your market is too small. You can likely do a yellow pages search and find hundreds of potential numbers to call in an instant. I taught you how to get a large leads list together in no time, so you'll have enough numbers to call for the next month. With the skills I'll be teaching you later in this book you'll learn how to leave the door open to contact people even if they aren't interested right now. By the time I'm done with you, you'll be deciding not to follow up with people because you'll have an abundance mentality, and the greener grass of fresh leads will be on the horizon.

It is an amazing feat to simply call through a leads list of 300 people—and most markets have tens of thousands of potential clients to speak to. Again, YOU WILL NEVER RUN OUT OF LEADS TO CALL.

The only small caveat is that you could feasibly run out of leads in your geographical area, which may be higher priority for you to call. Even so, you could just call the leads not in your area first to get practice before you call your local businesses.

Or, if you are calling current customers in your business, you may not have that many to reach out to. If this is the case, just practice on some cold leads first, and then eventually transition into the more important leads.

So now you can logically agree that you will not run out of people to call in the foreseeable future. So what's your problem? You are afraid of doing it wrong—which brings me to the other side of the scarcity coin, which is perfectionism.

Perfectionism

You think highly of yourself, and you have faith in the reasons you are calling. You just want to be perfectly ready before you start, to give yourself the best chances of success in your dialling endeavours.

Sorry to break it to you, but you are probably terrible at cold calling and will not get better until you fail your way to success.

Learning cold calling is a lot like learning a sport, like soccer.

You know it would be super cool to learn how to play soccer, and you decide you want to be the best player immediately. So you spend your time exercising and reading everything you can about the art of kicking a ball around. You become a soccer fanatic, spending months just reading about playing soccer, to get yourself ready for your big debut.

You have all the theoretical knowledge in your head and are ready to finally step onto the field. You're fit and know every soccer strategy in the book. Theoretically, you're a soccer genius—but how do you think you'll play?

Terribly. You will royally suck. You could have all the soccer knowledge in the world, but until you apply it you won't truly understand how to play the game.

Alternatively, imagine a different soccer scenario. You want to be an awesome soccer player, so you start reading all the material you can on it—but you also join a team to immediately apply your knowledge.

While you are reading the theoretical knowledge you are applying it at the same time. You would learn at a much more accelerated pace, and quickly outperform people who are learning how to play without the theoretical knowledge. As you are learning, you are testing it out and figuring out what works for you and what doesn't. You quickly you develop your own play style and become an amazing player. As you practice, you start to find weaknesses in your play style, and then you seek out specialized information to help you overcome these weaknesses quickly.

Knowledge only becomes power once you apply it. As you can tell, learning how to play a sport is a lot like learning how to cold call.

Your instincts will tell you that you're not ready yet, so you need to do more research, more reading, and more learning before you are ready. Unfortunately, you will never be "ready." Until you put what I teach you into practice, you will not really understand how the knowledge works for you. When you start applying what you learn, you suddenly start learning faster then you ever thought you could.

Trying to be perfect is a form of mental masturbation. It feels good, but doesn't really accomplish anything.

I want to encourage you to be imperfect. Start before you think you are fully prepared and accept that you'll burn through a couple leads before you start to get good. By the time you get though this book you will have a great system to start with, but it will still be far from perfect. You must remember that even though you aren't the best cold caller yet, you tried your best at the time with your current skill set, and learned from whatever happened in the call. The next call will be better because of your experience.

Just know that with all the basic knowledge I am giving you, I am trusting you to go out, practice it, and morph it into your own system. My goal isn't to make you the perfect caller—I just want to give you enough information to get you taking action in contacting your market. You must start calling even before you feel completely prepared, because that will help you learn faster. You will fail your way to success much more quickly if you start soon.

Now onto the biggest fear related to calling into your market—the R word.

Rejected!

MOST PEOPLE HAVE a fear of rejection, AKA a fear of their idea failing. The R word.

I define the fear of rejection as this: The fear that people will say no to you, reject your idea, or reject you as a person.

Rejection is a dish, often served cold, and it comes in a variety of flavors.

If you are hungry to learn, then you must be prepared to eat rejection for breakfast, lunch, and dinner—especially if you ever want to taste success in the future.

Food analogies aside, some people just won't be having it. No matter what you say, these people just won't want to talk to you. You could have a money tree that is guaranteed to grow millions in currency, hassle-free, and some people would tell you point blank that they have no use for it.

Don't take it personally, even though you might feel like you really should. Just know that you shouldn't. People are going to say no to you—a lot—and you are going to have to get used to it. Many people fear rejection, but what if I told you it was the best thing that could happen to you? Don't believe me? Well let's do a little thought exercise.

Exercise 2.2

I want you to think back on your life to a time when there was a high chance of rejection, but you faced it anyways. Try and remember how you felt when you knew there was a big chance of getting rejected and you faced it head on. Maybe it was taking the leap and applying for that awesome job that seemed unattainable. Maybe it was asking out that girl you had a huge crush on.

Here's an example from my past:

'I was doing research into the market for chiropractors in order to determine if they were looking for a new CRM solution. I created my leads list and started calling into my market, setting up meetings with chiropractors and sending out hundreds of emails. I had no experience trying to start a software business, but wanted to give it a try, learning as I went along. I was facing a lot of rejection from chiropractors. I felt a lot of pressure from my peers as well, as they were watching me try to start my own business. I was worried that if my idea failed, I would label myself a failure.'

Think of a time when you faced failure, the fear of rejection, or both. Write a sort paragraph about what you were thinking and feeling going into the situation, similar to my paragraph above.

When finished, answer these questions about the experience:

<u>What did you think was going to happen?</u>
<u>What actually happened?</u>
<u>Thoughts on the difference?</u>

Write it all down as you go through this process.

Take a look at how I answered these questions for my software business experience.

What I thought was going to happen:

In my software experience, I was convinced I was actually going to create a new software for chiropractors, but I was worried that, if I failed, my peers would look down on me. I thought I would just give up on being an entrepreneur if this failed. I thought it would crush my spirit.

What actually happened:

What actually happened was my idea did fail. After talking to an extensive number of chiropractors I found that the competition was too fierce to fit a new CRM product into the market. I ended up not creating the product, but learned a lot throughout the process. I told my peer group that I was not going to pursue that business opportunity anymore, and they congratulated me for trying. I found I was more motivated and ready to take on my next project after that experience. I didn't look at the venture as a failure, but rather a powerful learning experience that propelled me forward.

My thoughts on the difference:

I was very quick to disregard the positives that come from failure. It would have been great to start a software company, but the learning process that I went through was much more valuable than I could have known. My friends didn't reject me for failure, but rather praised me for giving it a champion's try. After I pulled the plug on my business idea, I became even more motivated to work on another business. Tasting the thrill of entrepreneurship was extremely addictive.

(Credit to my good friend Noam at www.lightwayofthinking.com for this exercise)

Now make sure you answer these questions about your experience.

Whether your experience ended in a win or a "learn," focus on the immense positives that came from chasing your vision.

— — — — — — — — —

Whatever your facing rejection story involves, it was probably one of your biggest achievements, and it probably felt really good. It was likely a defining moment in your life. Even if you failed in the end, you know you learned from the experience, and it made you a better person. What you are likely to find is that you vastly overestimated the bad that was going to happen. On the other side, the feelings of facing rejection and coming out on top was probably a huge positive experience for you. The small downside you faced was outweighed immensely by the lifelong benefits of facing your fears.

Ultimately, the fear of rejection is like a compass pointing you in the direction of personal development. When you feel scared of rejection, you know this is the path that will yield the most rewards. I have grown to like this fear, as it has driven me towards the most amazing experiences in my life.

That feeling of fear is really just a chemical reaction happening in your body. Your interpretation of it will define how it affects you. I'm getting a little meta here, but I want to inspire you to start thinking about this fear as something positive.

Now if only it were this simple to get you over your fear of rejection! But alas, fear is a clever beast. The fear of rejection has many disguises, and one of its most popular ones is the fear of your idea failing, (I.e., fear of people rejecting your idea).

Many people are afraid to start calling because they are worried that people won't like their product idea. This fear may not apply to you, but it applies to many people on the entrepreneurial path. They don't want any feedback on their amazing idea, because they are worried that people are going to tell them it's not so amazing.

Let's say hypothetically that you do find out that the idea is terrible and no one will buy it. It's much better to find this out as early as possible so that you can adjust or change the idea. Some people would rather stay blissfully ignorant and spend months developing products that nobody wanted in the first place. Meanwhile, if they had that feedback early on, they could have changed the trajectory of their businesses and avoided wasting time and money.

If I had not done this kind of research before creating a chiropractic business, I would have had a huge flop on my hands. Facing my fears and cold calling into my market allowed me to see the truth about whether I was pursuing a great business idea. If I had let this fear blind me, it would have caused a lot more damage to my finances later on.

Despite the many positives of facing your fears, people will find millions of excuses to not face the fear of cold calling:

- I'm not experienced enough yet.

- I need to work on my value proposition more.

- I'm not in the right headspace right now to try.

Watch for these rejection avoidance excuses, as they will disguise themselves as logic to fool you.

I'm willing to bet most of you reading this book are already thinking of reasons to avoid making any phone calls. You're only on chapter two, and you're already thinking, "Cold calling isn't for me, for reasons x, y, and z."

These thoughts are the fear of rejection disguising itself in logic. I'm sure that your <u>totally legitimate</u> excuses seem to make sense now—but then I have to ask, why are you reading this?

You found this material because this was a skill that you decided you needed, either for your business or personal pursuits. The skills you'll learn in this book will be applicable to many different areas of your business pursuits, so don't deprive yourself of that to avoid fear.

By facing rejection early on you will learn much more quickly then if you had avoided it, and it will make you immune to the fear, so much so that it will stop bothering you.

So to conclude, the fear of rejection is something you will face a lot going through this course. Facing rejection is one of the most awesome things you can do for your personal development. Depending on how you look at it, fear can be a form of motivation. Don't be tricked when this fear attempts to disguise itself as a reason to stop you from taking action, because the fear of rejection is very good at that. Fear of rejection is like a compass that points in the direction you must go for your own development.

Now that you're fearless, lets get you ready to start selling yourself. I mean pitching, of course.

CHAPTER Three:
Life's A Pitch

Ryan Mulvihill

Basic Pitches

THE FIRST THING you say to your prospect on the phone is what sets the tone for the rest of your conversation. They will know what to expect from your call, and can either comply or say no. Before you start calling, I want to get you ready to talk to real live strangers.

Starting a conversation with strangers is the area where the most people really mess up, as they make many wrong moves in the heat of the moment. There are three different types of pitches you will have to know for your cold calling: regular, elevator, and quick pitch. Each of these pitches has a slightly different use, and sometimes they are used in combination.

The regular pitch is your basic pitch—the pitch you will use if you know little about your prospect and you want to let them know why you're calling. The elevator pitch is a more detailed story about why you're calling them. You will be telling them a little about yourself and your business idea to pique their interest. Lastly, the quick pitch is a one-sentence pitch to immediately catch your client's attention, especially if you are in a pinch. In the final section of this chapter I'll teach you how to use each of these effectively. Let's take a closer look at each of them now.

Regular Pitch

I asked Jackson to do a practice pitch on me. I was about to help him put together his initial pitch and wanted to see what his baseline skill level was for calling.

We got into our positions, where he was going to pretend to call me and I was to play an interested customer. Nervously, Jackson held his hand up to his head, thumb and pinkie out in the shape of a telephone, as I did the same. "Ring ring," he said aloud.

"Hello, this is Ryan, owner of Ryan's Real Estate Company."

Jackson saw his cue to start pitching and explaining the intricate reasons for his call. Two minutes into his pitch, I had not been able to get a word in edgewise, other than grunts of acknowledgment.

Sensing my displeasure with his pitch, Jackson decided it was a good idea to talk faster and limit my chances to respond, while progressively getting more flustered. I had to break character, otherwise I would have had to endure this long-winded pitch going on for eternity. "Stop," I said, bringing his flustered speech to a dramatic end. It was going to be a long day of teaching him how to pitch, but I remembered that when I started I was naïve to the art of the pitch in the same way.

When I first began my foray into pitching cold prospects, I had a long and eloquent speech I was ready to give them. It was a real hero's journey, "Ryan's Odyssey," the story of a young entrepreneur trying to make the world a better place for reasons A, B, and C.

What I quickly realized, though, is that people just want you to get to the point so they can decide whether they want to continue the call with you. People have short attention spans and are easily confused.

What you initially say to your prospects sets the whole direction of the conversation. You need to be able to communicate your message as quickly as possible before you lose the little attention they afford you in the beginning. Keep the pitch simple—you don't want to confuse your prospect in the first few seconds of your call. You have roughly three sentences to quickly communicate these four things:

What is your <u>name</u>?
What is your <u>business or idea</u>?
<u>Why</u> are you calling me?
<u>What</u> do you want from the call?

So in practice, this would look something like this:

If you were researching a paid newsletter service for real estate agents:

"Hi, my name is Ryan (**Name**), and I'm considering starting up a newsletter service to help real estate agents keep in constant contact with their prospects (**Idea**). I see you are a real estate agent in the San Francisco area (**Why**), so I was wondering if I could run the idea by you and see if it is actually something that could help your business(**What**)?"

If you were doing market research on dentists:

"Hi, my name is Ryan (**Name**). I'm in a software development program (**Why**) and I'm looking to develop software to help dentists with challenges they face on a regular basis (**Idea**). I'm still doing research on what these challenges are, so I was hoping to ask you a few quick questions about your practice (**What**)."

Your pitches don't have to fit exactly into this format. These pitches are just examples of a basic way to effectively communicate your idea and grab your prospect's interest.

———————

Exercise 3.1

Create a pitch for your business idea in this format. Write out a few of them so you can see how different pitches flow for you. Write them out now.

When you have a couple prospective pitches, you will choose your favorite to practice with. You will practice by saying it out loud until you can belt it out without looking at your script. You may look like a crazy person doing it, but it's the only way to get used to pitching for the first time. Do this until your pitch comes out fluidly, without needing to look at your script.

On the surface it seems easy to create and execute your pitch, but this is an area where many people fumble. They get their pitch started and then forget one of their sentences partway through and end up rambling instead of delivering the pitch properly. This has to do with being nervous, and will be overcome with practice.

Beware the ROBO-Voice. When you practice saying your pitch for the first time, it may sound a bit robotic. Don't worry—as you are still becoming comfortable with the words you are saying, it will come off a little unnatural at first. With practice and repetition your pitch will eventually sound natural, just expect some growing pains.

We will practice getting your pitch right later in this chapter, but for now I just want you to get used to the sound of the words coming out of your mouth. Keep saying your pitch out loud until you are comfortable with it and it doesn't sound like the T-1000 terminator. It will be hard at first. Eventually your voice will sound full of energy again, after saying your lines about 40 times. After you are done, continue on.

—————————

Back to Jackson, the long-winded pitcher. By the end of the day he was his usual charming self on the telephone. After getting used to delivering his short pitch, he found people were usually very receptive to him.

This is the most standard of all the pitches, and will serve you well for most niches. However, when your prospect's attention is more limited, you may have to resort to the quick pitch.

SHORT AND SWEET

THIS IS FOR when you need to try and hook people with a single sentence. I learned this technique when I was trying to pitch SEO to escort companies.

Short Pitch

It started as a joke, but my business partner and I realized we had a very solid value proposition. There were tens of thousands of monthly searches for escort companies, so getting a certain company onto the first page of Google could be a huge business benefit. The only problem was actually getting these escort operators to listen to us.

"Hi, I'm Ryan calling from Jinx Digital. I was just calling different escort companies in Toronto to—" The click of the phone cut me off. That was the fifth escort operator who had hung up on me. Obviously my pitch technique wasn't working, and I decided to try something new. So I changed my strategy to try and capture their attention immediately.

"Hi, I was wondering if you were looking to get more people calling in to book escorts?" The operator paused for a moment, then said in a thick Russian accent, "Yes, I'd like that." "Great, just give me a minute to explain myself," I said nervously. Immediately I jumped into my elevator pitch and laid out why SEO made sense for this strange business niche. By the end of the day I had a couple of interested companies, and follow-up calls to make. If you want to read the whole hilarious story about my attempts at pitching escort companies, check out my blog post growanempire.com.

This experience taught me the power of the quick pitch, for when your target is being especially short with you on the phone. It is used to immediately create intrigue so that your prospect will grant you the chance to sell them. It is simply creating a sentence that will grab their attention, and that is related to your business proposition.

Here are a few examples of a solid quick pitch:

Hi [Name], are you interested in an easier way to keep in touch with your current contact list? (For a newsletter writer service.)

Are you interested in a fast and simple way to generate referrals and repeat business from your current clients? (Pitching a CRM solution.)

Do you want more customers calling in to book appointments with your business? (Pitching Internet marketing for dentists.)

I'm doing some research into the electrician market to create software to make your business run in half the time—mind if I ask you a few questions? (For doing market research or idea extraction on electricians.)

——————————

Exercise 3.2

Now try and put together a few of your own quick pitches for your product, service, or idea. Create a couple with different angles so you can play around with them to see what works. Focus on the immediate benefit someone will gain from talking to you right now. When you have a couple written out, practice saying them out loud, just like your regular pitch.

——————————

Now it is time to create the big one—the monster that is the elevator pitch.

ELEVATOR CONVERSATION

THIS TYPE OF pitch has surprisingly little to do with elevators and a lot to do with simply convincing your prospect that talking to you is a valuable use of their time. The elevator pitch is what you say when you're on an elevator and someone asks what you do. You have to answer before you reach your floor.

The Elevator Pitch

It's not really formulaic, like the other pitches—it is simply describing your idea or the value you bring to the table in roughly four sentences. This is enough to give your prospect an overview of what you offer, but not so much that you will bore them with the intricate details.

There are two main things that you need to keep in mind when developing your pitch. First, you need to know who you're talking to (i.e., try to use lingo that your niche would use, so you sound like you know what you're talking about). But at the same time, don't get too technical, as the person you're talking to may not be too adept in their industry. Keep it simple and make it easy to understand, even if who you're talking to isn't an expert.

Secondly, phrase your pitch in terms of what value you have to provide to them, not what you have to gain from this call. Nobody cares that this call would be really useful to you when it comes to developing your idea. But if you were to say that you could share some cool business tips you learned from other business owners, for example, then you have something to give.

Lastly, make sure to finish off your elevator pitch with a question to kick start the conversation. You need to lead so your prospect doesn't strain to continue the conversation. The elevator pitch can be comparable to your regular pitch, just with more detail in it.

Here are some examples of effective elevator pitches:

Elevator pitching your digital newsletter service:

"It's a digital magazine that you send to your contacts via personalized emails. It helps you stay on people's minds and builds your reputation as a trusted real estate adviser. The magazine contains content that is relevant to homeowners (apps for homeowners, travel, and productivity), along with areas for your personal branding, listings, and articles about the real estate market. It's a different concept from the typical digital newsletters you're probably familiar with. Does this sound like something you might have use for in your business?"

For someone doing research into the need for veterinarian software:

"Right now, I'm looking to develop a software application for veterinarians to help solve some of the challenges that they face on an ongoing basis. I have a couple of ideas that I think may excite you. Do you mind if I learn a little bit more about your business to see if there's anything I can do to help you?"

If they are receptive to this pitch, you would then have to explain your ideas during the conversation to get their feedback on what features are important to them.

Pitching a precise product to your industry:

"I'll tell you a little bit about our product. It's a wet umbrella bagger. Put simply, it is a machine that would sit in your lobby, and any guests that walk in with wet umbrellas would put them inside the machine to have them wrapped in plastic bag. This is used mostly to prevent slip and fall accidents and keep your lobby clean, and is another way to add to your guests' experience and convenience. Have you ever heard of a product like this before?"

—————————

Exercise 3.3

You guessed it—time to create your own elevator pitch. Use the examples above to craft one or two that work for you. Just like your regular pitch, I want you to practice them. The elevator pitch usually comes after the regular or quick pitch. It's your response to someone wanting more information about why you're calling, so phrase it as such.

When people are getting used to doing this sort of pitch, they like to really ramble. They get excited that a prospect has shown a little interest in what they are selling, and decide to try and give the prospect as much information as possible. Resist that urge. Keep your description short until they ask you to clarify certain areas. Remember, this is a conversation, not a monologue.

Now it is time to put all of your pitches together and create your pitch deck, which is your preparation for what you will say to your prospects when they first pick up the phone. It will contain the three pitches you created, but we will add an extra ingredient to spice things up. This extra ingredient is the "counter."

COUNTER ATTACK!

COUNTERS ARE SENTENCES that allow your conversation to flow smoothly when your prospect tries to throw a wrench into the cogs. Your counters are going to be very specific to your style of speech, so I'll just be giving you a few examples of how my script works to spark your imagination. If someone has an objection to some part of the call, the counter is what you will say to them. We'll get into creating a full on objection-counter list a bit later. For now you just need to know how to counter the most common objections.

Objections and Counters

Sometimes people are going to be a little hesitant to talk to you, and they'll throw out a little resistance. They are doing this to see if you are the real deal. If you can confidently handle their initial objection, then they will be much more willing to have a long call with you. The four most common objections you will face are the following:

I don't have time
Who are you?
What are you going to do with this information?
This is a strange approach.

To illustrate how to handle these objections skillfully, I want you to step into Nick's shoes. Nick has an idea for a service to help real estate agents keep in constant contact with their leads without being intrusive. In order to counter effectively, he has to insert his own charming personality into his counters while still pushing to get the conversation started. Here are examples of how to beat each of these objections, followed by some tips on how to do your own.

"I don't have much time right now."

"Just so you know, this call is on your schedule. It should only take 15 minutes. If, at any point, you need to run off and do something else, just let me know. I take no offence. Are you alright to have a quick conversation now, or do you want me to call back another time?"

When people say they don't have time right now, they are NOT saying they don't want to talk to you. It may simply be that they are busy at the moment. It may also be that they are afraid to commit to a lengthy call when they may need to run off. By taking the pressure off and assuring them the call is on their schedule, you make them feel more comfortable speaking to you. Then, by giving them the option of scheduling the call for a different time, you have a possibility of setting up a lengthy call with them in the near future. The time constraint objection is extremely easy to handle if you know how.

"Who are you?"

"I have years of experience coding and am good friends with a realtor. He mentioned some of the business problems he was facing and I wanted to help. Right now I'm researching a bunch of possible problems I can solve in the real estate industry. This is just a call to explore your business and see if the solution I've been working on might be right for you."

Some people get scared when a prospect asks this question because they don't understand what the prospect is really saying. Usually the prospect is just trying to find out if you are with some large company and doing some sneaky sales pitch to trick them into a conversation. All you have to do to counter this is convey that you are an authentic entrepreneur, share a tidbit of your backstory, and tell them why it makes sense to call them. They just want a little assurance that you are not a sleazy salesperson or scam artist.

"What are you going to do with the information?"
"Exactly how I use the information will depend on what we find out in the call. It could be as simple as a follow-up email with some resources, an introduction to someone else, or perhaps even creating a full-blown product to help out real estate agents like you. My intention is to help you build your business in whatever way I can. Right now I'm researching a business idea to see if it is something that could really help you out. However, if this conversation helps me to think of any other way to benefit your business, I will do what I can to help you out."

This objection rarely comes up, but you should be prepared for it. Don't just tell them what you plan to do with information you get from them —tell them how it benefits them to talk to you. You aren't just gathering information selfishly, you are going to be sharing the information to make people's businesses better. By telling them the benefits to sharing information, you will get much longer and more detailed conversations from your prospects.

"This is such a strange approach."

"I agree—this is definitely a strange way to research a business idea. But I want to learn as much as I can from other real estate agents to eventually develop the best possible product for them. My intention is to create something that will really help out your business, so I want to talk to as many real estate agents as possible to help me create something really awesome. Worst-case scenario I can share some of the tips I learned from my research into the market to help you out."

Some people are a little put off by your call because they've never experienced something like this before. Entrepreneurs talking to their markets before they develop businesses? That is madness! Except it's not. It's the best way to create something your customers will really like. So if someone asks you why you are making calls like this, you can confidently say you are doing it to take the smart approach to starting a business.

—————————

Exercise 3.4

You are now going to take each of these objections and create your own counters for them. The examples I've written above fit the way I speak, and flow naturally for me. You need to make a counter that flows naturally for you. Use my examples to help you along in crafting your own counters.

Create a counter for each of these objections:

"Who are you?"

"I don't have much time right now."

"What are you going to do with the information?"

"This is such a strange approach."

— — — — — — — — —

These are the most common objections you will hear when you start calling. Simply knowing how you will counter them will make you more confident in building your calling script. Now that you have your pitches figured out, you can make your very first pitch deck!

MAKE YOUR PITCH DECK

YOUR PITCH DECK is going to be the first building block of your whole sales formula. It focuses on how you are going to pitch to your prospect and what that conversation is going to look like at first. All you are doing is taking the pitches you created, putting them all together in a document, and making a battle plan for how people are likely to respond. I even added a little extra to some pitches to make them flow better, like mentioning that the call will only take a few minutes.

I'll give you an example of what a pitch deck will look like, and add in some transitions. Transitions are what you say after a pitch to flow into conversation naturally. We will be following the example of Nick researching his paid newsletter service in the real estate agent market. Your deck will be unique to you, but it will follow my basic formula. Simply swap all of the information I have below into your own sheet.

Nick's Pitch Deck

Regular pitch
"Hi, my name is Nick. I'm considering starting up a newsletter service to help real estate agents keep in constant contact with their

prospects. I see you are a real estate agent in the San Francisco area, so I was wondering if I could run the idea by you and see if it is actually something that could help your business? It'll only take a couple of minutes."

- After you deliver your pitch, there are two ways your prospect may respond.
- If they offer compliance—"OK, let's do it"—then you deliver your elevator pitch.
- If they have an objection—"I'm not sure I have time"—then counter. If they comply with your counter, go to your elevator pitch.

Quick Pitches

"Hi [Name]. This is Nick. I'm calling to see if you're interested in finding an easier way to keep in touch with your current contact list."

"Hey [Name]. Are you interested in keeping in contact with all your potential leads in an easy non-obtrusive way?"

"Hi [Name], I'm curious, do you keep in regular contact with your prospects and clients?"

Common responses to quick pitches:
"Sounds interesting. What is it about?" – Go into elevator pitch.
"Who are you and why are you calling?" – Say,"Let me just quickly explain myself." Then go into regular pitch.
They have an objection. – Counter, and then go into elevator pitch.

Elevator Pitch

"It's a digital magazine that you send to your contacts via personalized emails. It helps you stay on people's minds and builds your reputation as a trusted real estate adviser. The magazine contains content that is relevant to homeowners (apps for homeowners, travel, and productivity), along with areas for your personal branding, listings, and articles about the real estate market. It's a different concept from the typical digital newsletters you're probably familiar with. Does this sound like something you might have use for in your business?"

— — — — — — — — —

Exercise 3.5

Create your own pitch deck in the format above. You can change it around depending on how you are pitching your market, and what market you are pitching to. Don't just swap out my words—make this pitch deck your own. Insert your regular pitch, quick pitch, and elevator pitch and then write out the counters to the objections I've shown you. Use words you are comfortable with, because it will make your calling much easier. Start writing!

— — — — — — — — —

What you are doing is creating a document I call a "Cold Call Battle Plan" to help you out during your calls. The pitch deck is the first piece of this puzzle. By the end of this book you will have a whole strategy for calling your target market and getting the information you need to know if your business idea is a possible success. It is vital that you actually do the work and write out all of this information. That way you will know your strategy inside and out when you are calling, and you will speak confidently on the phone. You may know your calling strategy so well that you will never actually have to look at your Cold Call Battle Plan. That would be great! Unfortunately, you won't get to that level until you actually create this document. So put in the work and follow the exercises—your calls will go so much better if you do.

To wrap up your pitch deck, remember this: I could give you a million and one ways to pitch your prospects, but it won't really help. Crafting the best pitch for cold calling is something that you have to test over a period of time. Practice the regular pitch, quick pitch, elevator pitch, or any other pitch you can think of to grab your prospect's attention.

I encourage you to try your own spins on the pitches I've shown you. Your pitch will evolve as you do your calls, so don't worry about getting it right the first time. You will get better the more practice and experience you get. Your pitch deck is the seed your beautiful call script will blossom from. It is just one part of the Cold Call Battle Plan.

I figured out these pitching formulas after years of calling, and they worked for me. I was terrible when I first started. Expect pitching to be a little awkward at first. I'm just here to make the process as smooth as possible.

Now that you have a pitch deck worked out, you can start to think of what you will say after they agree to take a call with you. That will lead us to the hierarchy, the meat of your phone call.

Chapter Four: The Hierarchy

Ryan Mulvihill

What Do You Want?

I WANT TO start off by saying that I do not want to turn you into a robot, one who reads lines off of a script, where every answer a customer gives you is just the next step down a decision tree. But my thinking didn't start like this.

When I initially started teaching people the art of cold calling I was tempted to do this, as it just seemed easier. Create a structured calling script and tell the person to follow the script—cold call training done, right? If only life were so simple. My initial training sessions were very frustrating.

My students, who were normally witty fun people to talk to, would turn into automatons on the phone. When they followed my script they would lose all sense of humor and wit in their calls. This made me remember why it was so uncomfortable to talk to normal telemarketers. Whatever you said, you had the feeling that you were just working your way down their call tree. They weren't so much listening to you as simply gauging your response in reference to their script.

For fear of my trainees sounding like they're pitching free cruises from a call center in India, I realized I had to change things up. I needed a system that would keep cold callers on track, but still leave them the flexibility to have engaging conversations.

I'm not going to create some sort of flow chart like telemarketers have. Instead, I'm going to give you a flexible system that you can fall back on to make your calls run really smoothly. The process is more organic like that. There are some scripted lines you will prepare, but they are there to help guide you, not to force your conversations in one direction. I will teach you to rely more on your intuition then on your script.

Think of me as a mixed martial arts (MMA) teacher, showing you a bunch of different moves for different situations. Laying out a fight from start to finish would be impossible, as your opponent could react in an infinite number of ways. The best way to prepare for this fight would be to learn a bunch of moves that can be applied when you need them to be. I'll teach you the mindset of a fight, so you can think on your feet and still react effectively to your opponent.

This is the central philosophy of Cold Call Karate—learning to have fluid conversations with prospects you've never met, to learn whether your business idea is a win or not.

So if you want to get something out of the call, you have to know what you want. It sounds like a simple idea, but this is where most people have trouble. They know that their end goal is to find out if people will buy their business idea, but they don't know what other things could really benefit them along the way.

In order to get everything you want out of a call with a prospect, you need to know everything you CAN get. This is the base of the hierarchy—having a list of everything you can get out of a call, and knowing how to get it.

The problem is that most people think of cold calling as a yes or no situation. It is anything but. There are a bunch of different possibilities of what could happen. In order to make sure you are maximizing the value of each phone call, make sure you have a list of everything you can get out of the phone call.

This is the basis of the hierarchy—knowing your priorities for a call.

We'll be taking those priorities and turning them into an awesome call strategy, but for now just focus on one simple question.

What do you want?

When you are testing out your business idea you will have a number of opportunities that can present themselves if you are looking for them.

- Maybe a local business will be open to meeting you in person to discuss your business idea.
- Maybe a prospect will want to be added to an email list to be updated on your businesses progression.
- Maybe a prospect will be open to talking to you out of work hours to tell you exactly what they would want from your business idea.
- Maybe a prospect knows someone in their industry who would be very interested in your business idea.

Don't look at these calls as a way to get a single yes or no answer on whether they like your business idea—look at them as a way to really connect with your potential market.

When it comes to actually making these calls, you have to think of all the things you could get from a target. Depending on the market you are targeting and the reason for calling, your hierarchy could look very different from someone else's.

———————

Exercise 4.1

So right now we are going to write down your hierarchy, which will be based on a couple of different factors.

What is the best-case scenario of your call?

What if they say no? What's the next best thing?

What if they say no to that? What's the next best thing?

Next, ask the following question:

If this person says yes to some of these inquiries, then what else can I get from them?

What connections might they have? What would I want to know about them? Would they be willing to buy more?

Write your hierarchy into a list of outcomes, rather than fully explaining each scenario. List out every possible bit of value that could possibly come out of a phone call. Be as thorough as possible. By the end of this exercise you should have a hierarchy that resembles this basic framework:

<u>Target</u>
1. Sell your product.
2. Schedule in-person meet-up.
3. Schedule a sales call.
4. Successful interview call*.
5. Scheduled interview call*.

6. Call back in a week/month.
7. Referral.
8. Email.
9. Call another time?

Seriously, I want you to write out your hierarchy right now. Don't worry about getting it perfect—just try to get your first draft done.

Keep asking this question until you can't come up with anything of value the person on the phone can give you. Scrape the bottom of the bucket for value. Even if this person says no to every proposition you give them, they will probably still give you their email to send some information to. If this person said no to every previous question, they will probably not respond to an email you send them—but that isn't the point. You won't always get what you want, but you will become comfortable with pushing for what you want.

*A point to clarify here is the "interview call" part of the hierarchy. The interview can be a set of prepared questions you want to ask your market. Maybe you want to find out what blogs they look to for advice on their business; maybe you want to find out about what areas of their business is frustrating for them; maybe you want to run your idea by them in depth to figure out new features you could be adding to it. The interview portion is an important step in your hierarchy, but don't worry about what questions you'll be asking. We'll get into that a bit later.

――――――――――

Exercise 4.2

Now this may sound a little strange, but I want you to make a second hierarchy, for the gatekeeper.

The gatekeeper is the person who often stands between you and your target. They are the office secretaries, the assistants, the relayers of messages, and often your worst enemies. But they can be useful if you know what they can provide.

Ask the same hierarchy questions. What is the best-case scenario when talking to a gatekeeper? Next best? Work you way down until you have something like this:

Gatekeeper
1. Puts you through to your target.
2. Puts you through to your target's equivalent*.
3. Gives you a better time to call back.
4. Gives you a target's email.
5. Lets you leave a voicemail message for your target.

*Depending on your market, there may be multiple people in the office who are able to give you the feedback and information you need. We will take chiropractors, for example. Maybe the main chiropractor isn't in the office, but you could probably gain a ton of great feedback from one of the assistant chiropractors.

— — — — — — — — —

Here are two examples of hierarchies for different situations. Yours should look something like these:

Researching a software idea for dentists

Prospect

Interested in signing up for trial when demo is ready.

Interested in meeting up to discuss idea.

Interview in desired software features.

Scheduled interview call.

Referral to someone else in the industry.

Schedule a follow-up call.

Get email to send updates/newsletter about your idea.

Undefined call-back time

Gatekeeper

Put me through to target.

Put me through to a dental assistant or office assistant.

Call back at set time to reach target.

Gives me target's email.

Lets me leave a voicemail with the target.

Leave a message with gatekeeper.

Gauging interest on selling a custom massage kit to yoga studios

Prospect

Schedule in-person meet-up to discuss product features.

Interview call on what they would want from the kit.

Scheduled interview call.

Referral to someone else in the industry.

Schedule follow-up call when they are free.

Sign them up for a newsletter to follow development of your idea.

Get email to send basic information.

Undefined call-back time.

Gatekeeper

Puts me through to business owner.

Puts me through to any yoga instructor.

Call back at set time to reach target.

Gives me target's email.

Lets me leave target a voicemail.

Leave a message with the gatekeeper.

Once you have your hierarchy written out, continue on to the next section. We are going to take your hierarchy and turn it into something awesome. You know what you want—now how are you going to get it?

You Never Get If You Never Ask

NOW WE ARE going to turn that hierarchy into your calling script. Remember, I don't want to turn you into a robot that follows a script—but going into a call without any forethought will cause you to stumble. What we are going to do is create lead-in sentences for all the steps in your hierarchy. You are going to craft the best way to ask for each of the things on your hierarchy. This way, when you want to ask a prospect if they would like to meet up, you won't sound like a nervous teenager asking his crush to prom. Crafting these lead-in sentences will make your conversations as smooth as the cream cheese on your bagel. You'll know how to move conversations forward when you want to, and have a higher likelihood of getting what you want from a call.

Let's assume you have an idea for a new software product that can help out dentists. You have a pretty good idea of the features dentists need, but you'd still like some feedback on your product idea. Your main goal is to get them to agree to be on your beta test list for when you launch. This is what your hierarchy would look like, taken from the previous section:

Prospect
- Interested in signing up for trial when demo is ready.

- Interested in meeting up to discuss idea.
- Interview on desired software features.
- Scheduled interview call.
- Referral to someone else in the industry.
- Schedule a follow-up call.
- Get email to send updates on your idea to.
- Undefined call-back time.

Gatekeeper
- Puts you through to target.
- Puts you through to a dental assistant or office assistant.
- Call back at set time to reach target.
- Gives you target's email.
- Lets you leave a voicemail with the target.
- Leave a message with gatekeeper.

In order to have a chance at getting your desired outcomes, you have to know how to ask for them. We are going to take each of these outcomes and turn them into lead-in questions.

Exercise 4.3

So now we are going to take each desired outcome in this process and write a sentence to ask for it. You don't have to get too fancy with your asking sentences—just write them in a way you would be comfortable speaking. For example, if one of your outcomes is to get coffee with the person, it would look like this:

Schedule coffee meet-up:

"Thanks for taking the time to hear about my idea. You seem really knowledgeable about your industry. I'd love to grab coffee sometime this week and talk more. What's your schedule look like?"

Don't worry about getting the sentences exactly right—I just want you to give it your best try. The sentences will likely change a bit in the next step of this process.

Remember that this will be after you say your elevator pitch, so your target will know what you are calling about. Right now you are trying to move the call forward to your desired outcomes.

I want you to create these for both your prospect and gatekeeper hierarchies. I took the hierarchy from before and wrote out a proper lead-in sentence for each point. Here are a bunch of examples of asking sentences for all the parts of the hierarchy to help you out in creating your own.

Target Hierarchy Sentences

Interested in signing up for trial when demo is ready:

"From what I've told you about my product idea, if it did everything we talked about, would this be something you'd be interested in demoing eventually?"

Interested in meeting up to discuss idea:

"I've had a great time talking with you. Is there any way that we could meet up sometime this week or the next, or I could take you out for coffee so I could learn more about how I can make this software really useful to dentists?"

Interview on desired software features:

"I'm looking for feedback on some of the aspects of my software. Do you mind if I run some of them by you, and you can give me your feedback on it?"

*Here you could ask questions like how much would you pay for the software, do you need feature x, how does your payment system work, etc. I will get into creating interview questions in the next section.

Scheduled interview on current software ideas:

"Is there a time this week when I could give you a call back so I could run a few ideas by you? I want to make sure my software is a huge help to dentists."

Referral to someone else in the industry:

"Do you know any other dentists off the top of your head that you could recommend to me to have the same kind of conversation with?"

Email Subscription:

"I'd like to keep in touch with all of the dentists that I'm speaking with. Do you mind if I grab your email to send you a weekly update as this software idea evolves?"

Schedule a follow-up call:

"Hey [First Name], thanks for taking the time to talk to me. I know you're really busy. Would you be open to me giving you a call back in [general timeframe] to pick your brain a little bit more?"

Schedule a call-back time:

"Is there a time today or this week when I could give you a call back when you wouldn't be as busy?"

Email contact:

"Hey, I know you're busy right now. Do you mind if I send you a quick email to tell you about my software idea? You could look it over in your spare time. Then I could call you back in a week or two and follow up with you."

Undefined call-back time

"Would you be open to me calling back in a few weeks to check in and see if you are interested in the developments I've made?"

Gatekeeper Hierarchy Sentences

Put you through to target:

"Hey, could you put me through to (dentist's first name)?"

Put you through to someone equivalent:

"That's alright if (main dentist) is busy. Are there any other dentists around that I could have a quick word with?"

Call back at set time:

"Is there a better time I could call back when (main dentist) will be in the office?"

Email:

"Is there an email I can reach (main dentist) at?"

Voicemail:

"Could you put me through to his voicemail?"

Leave a message with gatekeeper:

"Could you leave him this message?"

Don't just copy my example sentences—work to create asking sentences that work for you. You have a different flow of speaking than I do, so use that to create your asking sentences. Write a sentence that flows naturally for you and your type of speech.

— — — — — — — — —

Now that you have your asking sentences prepared, we are going to rearrange them in a way so you will be able to use them more easily when you are on a call with someone. We are going to figure out the flow of the conversation to make it easier for you to talk to your prospects. First, however, we need to come up with a few interview questions.

What Do I Want to Learn?

IN THE PREVIOUS section I mentioned interview questions. Simply put, these are the questions you would want to ask to learn more about your market. I learned a majority of these questions while going through an entrepreneurial course called "The Foundation." I call them interview questions because you are basically interviewing your prospect on your business idea or their industry.

Here are some basic examples of interview questions:

- How much would you pay for a product like this?
- Have you ever heard about anything like this in your industry?
- What sort of features would you need for this product?
- Would you be willing to pre-pay for this product to help fund its development?
- How much would it be worth to you if this product saved you four hours of work per week?
- Do you currently pay for any software?

Your interview questions will be unique to you, depending on how developed your business idea is.

A client I was coaching wanted to white-label some folding purse hooks that he was ordering from China and sell them to fashion boutiques. He had questions relating to the type of material people wanted, whether they had seen this product in other stores, and how much they would pay for it.

Another client I was coaching had an already-developed software to help out lawyers with tracking the time they spent on emails in order to bill clients more effectively. She had specific questions about how much their time was worth and how much revenue they were missing out on by not implementing this software.

Exercise 4.4

I want you to brainstorm a couple of different interview question ideas. Just think of every possible thing you want to learn about the market, and write it down as a question.

Don't hold back! Write down every thing you've ever wondered about your target market and create a question about it. You could read books and Wikipedia articles to learn about your market, or you could just ask them a few questions.

The whole point of this process is to learn very quickly about your market, so don't bog yourself down with research. Just pick up the phone and call some people.

After you have at least five good questions written down, prioritize them. Figure out which is the number one question you need the answer to. Then organize your questions according to priority. This way, when you are actually doing your calls and have limited time, you will ask the most important questions first.

Startup Idea Action Plan

Now that you have your interview questions worked out, you can add them into your Cold Call Battle Plan in the next section.

When Do I Ask?

SO YOU KNOW what you want to get from the calls and you know how to ask for it—now you just need to know WHEN to ask for it.

What we are going to do is lay out all your sentences in the order you may ask them, and retool them to make sense. Going off the previous example, you are still a software developer with an idea for a dental clinic management software. You are looking to find people who would be open to the software when it is ready and learn from your market about other features they want the software to have.

Imagine you are calling a dental office to pitch your software. How would the conversation flow? What points would you like to bring up first? Who would you be talking to first? Take these into account while you are creating your call flow. Keep in mind that, due to the nature of cold calling, you may have limited time on the call, so you are going to want to ask your top priority questions first.

That being said, you cannot lead with: "Do you want to buy this product?" You need to engage your prospect before you ask the big ticket question. The easiest way to engage your prospect is to ask your interview questions first. You don't need to go through all of the questions—just enough to get them in an engaged conversation. A few of the interview questions will warm them up to answering the harder hitting questions.

Exercise 4.5

Map out how you think a basic conversation would flow, similar to the example below. You don't need to write the rationale like I have for each of the sentences, just write the lead-in sentences themselves. These are to get you prepared for the twists and turns of a conversation with your prospect. It will not be a script you have to follow word for word, it's just a basic outline of how you think conversations will go. Use the language you would be comfortable saying in your script, bearing in mind that the way I speak is probably very different from how you would phrase things.

Morph your hierarchy into something like what I have below. Focus on creating a flow for your conversation. Make all your questions work into a basic conversation like I have. The sentences where I explain my rational for each part of this script are just there to help you follow along easily and create your own.

Basic Calling Script Gatekeeper

When you call the dental office, the first person you will likely talk to is a secretary. You should first ask to be put through to the main dentist.

Put me through to target:

"Hey, could you put me through to (dentist's first name)?"

If they're not in, you would then ask to be put through to any other dentist working there.

Put you through to someone equivalent:

"That's alright if (main dentist) is busy. Are there any other dentists around that I could have a quick word with?"

If all the dentists are busy, you will likely want to find a time to call back when they're not busy.

Call back at set time:

"Is there a better time I could call back when (main dentist) will be in the office?"

Regardless of being busy or not, you will probably want to try and grab the main dentist's email so you can try and reach out to him/her online.

Email:

"Is there an email where I can reach (main dentist) at?"

If there is no chance to reach the dentist by calling, you could try and leave a voicemail.

Voicemail:

"Could you put me through to his voicemail?" Then, when you get through to voicemail, deliver a pitch to build some intrigue. It will probably look similar to your standard pitch, with a prompt to call you back. It would look something like this:

"Hi, my name is Ryan. I'm developing software to help dentists reduce slippage and keep in touch with their client base. I'm still doing research on what the market needs, so I was hoping to ask you a few quick questions about your practice. When you get a chance, call me back at 555-555-5555. Hope to speak to you soon."

Leave a message with gatekeeper:

"Could you leave (dentist's name) this message?" If the secretary won't give you an option to leave the dentist a VM, then you could ask her to pass along a message like this:

"I'm Ryan, and I'm developing software called DENTSchedule. It's designed to help dentists reduce slippage and keep in touch with their client base. I'm still doing research on what the market needs, so I was hoping to ask you a few quick questions about your practice. When you get a chance, call me back at 555-555-5555. Hope to speak to you soon."

Basic Calling Script Target

Now, when you get put through to one of your targets, you should pitch them like you planned in the pitch section. For the sake of simplicity, I will just put in the regular and elevator pitch. You can get an entire example cold call battle plan here at growanempire.com/resources.

Start of conversation

"Hi, is this (target's name)?"

"Yes, it is."

"Hi, my name is Ryan. I'm in a software development program, and I'm looking to develop software to help dentists with challenges they face on a regular basis, specifically regarding client slippage. I'm still doing research on what kind of features dental practices would need in this software. Mind if I get your feedback on the idea?"

If they offer compliance—"OK, let's do it"—then you deliver your elevator pitch.

If they have an objection—e.g., "I'm not sure I have time"—then counter. If they comply with the counter, go to the elevator pitch.

Elevator Pitch

"I have been doing some research into the dental industry, and have realized just how costly patient slippage is. One patient is worth hundreds of dollars a year to a dental practice, so if you lose one it represents a big cost. So I've dreamed up software that you can load all your current clients into that will keep track of people who miss appointments. It will automatically email delinquent clients to prompt them to book an appointment. I'm also thinking of having a feature that reminds your secretary to call clients who have missed appointments, to try and get them new appointments. That's my basic plan for this software that I'm considering building."

This is the point of the conversation that you can't really plan for. Depending on your prospect, they may start asking you questions, and the conversation will start to flow from here. Maybe they want to know a little more about you. Maybe they want to dig a bit deeper into your idea. Maybe they will throw an objection your way. Talk to them, answer their initial questions, and when you feel you have built enough comfort to move the conversation towards the hierarchy questions, go ahead and ask them. You will likely try and ask your highest priority questions first.

Interview on current software ideas:

"I'm looking for feedback on some of the aspects of my software. Do you mind if I run some of them by you and you can give me your feedback on it?"

* Here you could ask questions like how much would you pay for the software, do you need feature x, how does your payment process work, etc.

Question examples include:

- How much would you pay for a product like this?
- Have you ever heard about anything like this in your industry?
- What sort of features would you need for this product?
- Would you be willing to pre-pay for this product to help fund its development?

If they're to busy at the moment to speak with you at length, you could try and schedule a call with them another time.

Interested in a demo:

"From what I've told you about this idea so far, if it did everything I talked about, would this be something you'd be interested in demoing in your dental office?"

You'd likely follow up this question with a why/why not question. After you gauge their interest, it may be a good transition into asking for feedback on your general product idea. Most business owners won't be able to give you an accurate answer to this question UNTIL you have probed them with some interview questions. When they understand the pain you are solving they can put a price tag on it. A dentist may not think your software that can reduce slippage is very useful unless he realizes how much revenue each patient brings in, and how much he is loosing when they slip away.

Scheduled interview on current software ideas:

"I totally understand you're busy right now. Is there a time this week when I could give you a call back so I could run a few ideas by you? I want to make sure my software is a huge help to dentists."

Now that you have some feedback on your product, you probably know if you would like to meet your target in person.

In-person meet-up:

"Thanks for all the feedback you've given me. You sound very knowledgeable about the industry. Is there any way that we could meet up sometime this week or the next, or I could swing by your office so I could learn more your practice?"

If they talk to you in length and seem really engaged with you, then around now would be a good time to ask for a referral.

Referral:

"Thanks for all the feedback you've given me. I'm trying to speak to as many dentists as possible to make an awesome product. Do you know any other dentists off the top of your head that you could recommend to have the same kind of conversation with?"

Even if you have their email, you should ask them if they are alright with you sending them updates on your product. This will keep lines of communication open and start building your email list.

Email subscription:

"I'd like to keep in touch with all of the dentists that I'm speaking with. Do you mind if I grab your email to send you a weekly update on the development of my software?"

If you had a great conversation with your target, you will probably want to talk to them again in the future. Or maybe they have to get off the phone to solve a dental issue. Just give them this line to setup another time to talk to them.

Schedule a follow-up call:

"Hey [First Name], thanks for taking the time to talk to me. I know you're really busy. Would you be open to me giving you a call back in [general timeframe] to pick your brain a little bit more (or get more feedback on my project as it develops)?"

And if you can't lock them down to a certain time to speak to them, you could say this to keep the lines of communication open (it's very non-committal, so most people will be fine with you calling them back at an undefined time).

Undefined call-back time:

"Would you be open to me calling back in a few weeks to check in and see if you might need it later?"

If they don't want you to call them back, then don't take it personally. Some people just aren't having it, even if they had a full-on conversation with you.

―――――――――

This is your battle strategy, but it is far from a perfect plan. This is not something for you to read out like you're a robot. It's more of a path to follow, even if you stray from it now and then. That is fine, because whenever the conversation gets off track you can refer back to your lead-in sentences.

When you want to move the conversation in another direction, or try and ask for something new, then these lead-in sentences will stop you from fumbling. You don't need to waste your mental energy on trying to figure out how to phrase a sentence. Just focus on execution.

Sometimes conversations will take twists and turns that completely throw your plan out of whack.

That is OK.

Just know that you now have a basic plan for asking for everything you need from a prospect. You are poised to get as much value as possible from a call with your prospect.

Now what you are probably worried about is "What if they say no?"

Well, let's plan for some objections. This brings me back to my window cleaning days, when I was facing objections multiple times a day. It became a competition between us window cleaning managers to figure out the best counters to every objection. We're going to apply this can-do attitude to your business prospects so you can get what you want from them.

SCARING SECRETARIES

A WORD ON gatekeepers, for the soon to be callers. Don't be intimidated by the secretaries—it is your job to intimidate them. Allow me to explain.

Take a look at the call script I have laid out for gatekeepers. It seems pretty bare bones, right?

Basic Calling Script Gatekeeper
Put you through to target:
"Hey, could you put me through to (dentist's first name)?"
Put you through to someone equivalent:
"That's alright if (main dentist) is busy. Are there any other dentists around that I could have a quick word with?"
Call back at set time:
"Is there a better time I could call back when (main dentist) will be in the office?"
Email:
"Is there an email I can reach (main dentist) at?"

The first thing you say to the gatekeeper will either set you up for success or set you up for failure when it comes to getting past them. Their job as a gatekeeper is to keep you out. They don't know that you are a good guy looking to help out their market by developing an awesome product. They will simply put you in the bucket of "salesperson" and never let you speak to a decision maker. That's just not very nice.

Most people's first reaction, when faced with a gatekeeper, is to try and win them over. They want to explain exactly why they are trying to reach the prospect in hopes that the gatekeeper will become their personal cheerleader. My advice is: Don't bother. Rarely do they care enough to give you a hand, and often they will just blow you off. In order to get past the gatekeeper, you have to adopt a different mindset and tone of voice.

You have to become a bit of an asshole to conquer the gatekeeper. You have to imagine that the gatekeeper is wasting YOUR time by not putting you through to your target. When the gatekeeper picks up the phone, they will say something like:

"Hi, you've reached Valley Dentists. Jessica speaking, how can I help you?"

And you must respond, in an almost angry voice:

"Hey, can you put me through to James?"

You only say his first name in order to signal a level of familiarity with James, even though he is just a name on your list. You also have to sound a little pissed off that they are holding you up. You have important business to discuss with this James character. Usually they will realize they have to put you through, as you sound serious. On occasion, though, they will question you. "Who can I tell him is calling?" they will ask, hoping to soften you up. "This is Ryan," you will respond, sounding just as agitated.

Now the gatekeeper will often relent and just put you through to your prospect, but on occasion they will have the audacity to question you again.

"What is this regarding?" they will ask gingerly.

"I'm calling to follow up on an email I sent him. Is he in the office?" you say in your best agitated voice. Now if they don't put you through to James, then they are the toughest of gatekeepers and you have almost no hope of getting by them. However, most of the time they will put you through no problem.

Most people I've taught this process to don't believe that it actually works. They think "No way a gatekeeper is going to put an angry customer through to their boss!" Unfortunately for the bosses out there, it does work. Gatekeepers know their bosses are much more adept at handling customer issues then they are so they WILL put you through. I could keep telling you logical reasons as to why this works, but you won't believe how well it works until you try it. Be OK with being just a little bit mean.

Don't feel bad about coming off a little tough on the gatekeepers — it's just what you have to do. They are often very nice people whom I would love to go out for tea with. In the long run you are helping them by researching a business idea that could really help out their workplace. They should be thanking you for the call, and admiring your entrepreneurial initiative. Unfortunately they have been told not put any salespeople through to the manager, and if you were to soften up you would sound a lot like one of those salespeople.

If the aggressive doesn't work and they force you explain why you are calling, then you can soften up and give them your elevator pitch. However, only use this as a last resort, because at that point it is unlikely you will be getting through to your prospect.

Now that your conscience is clear, we should think about the objections your prospect may bring up during the call.

Objections, Your Honor!

IT IS THE ninja move of all cold callers—the art of deflection. It's how to deflect a no and push for a yes, without coming off as sleazy. You will learn to crush objections by gently sweeping them away. It is much easier for someone to say no than it is to say yes. These moves are going to make it harder to say no to you. Sometimes your prospect won't give you a hard no, but will rather take the conversation in a direction you don't want it to go. You need to keep things on track and get as much value as possible out of the phone call.

I used to give up much too easily on my cold calls before I learned to use deflection. My prospects would bring the conversation to a close or give me an objection, and I would treat the call like a lost cause. Being good at deflection gives you back control of the conversation. It allows you to push for what you want without coming off as the sleazy car salesman. People don't mind you pushing for what YOU want on a call, as long as you are smooth about it. Deflection is all about being smooth.

You will be using deflection to counter any objections you face when you are doing cold calling. Although not all of your objection counters are going to follow this exact form, it is the basis that you will be building your objection list off of.

The steps for deflection are:
1. Validate what they said.
2. Sympathize with them.
3. Push from a slightly different angle and/or handle their objection.

Here is an example of this in action:

You are a window cleaner trying to book a customer over the phone:

You: When would you like to get your windows cleaned?

Prospect: Oh, getting them cleaned is so far in the future I really can't decide on that right now.

You: I totally understand (validate). Your schedule is crazy and you have no idea what you will be doing in the future (sympathize). What we can do is set up a tentative date and then I'll call you a week before to confirm. If you need to change or cancel, I totally understand. Around when would be a good time to get your windows cleaned (push)?

You are doing market research in the dental industry and trying to do an idea extraction.

You: I'm calling to speak to Nick.

Prospect: Dr. Nick isn't in today. I can leave him a message for you.

You: Yeah, we could definitely do that (validate). I understand that he is a very busy doctor (sympathize). Maybe instead I could speak to one of the other doctors in the clinic, or call back at another time when he is in the office (push)?

When someone brings the conversation to a conclusion or an area you are not happy with, take back control by deflecting the conversation.

Validate what they say, sympathize with the statement, and then push the conversation in the direction you want. It will be a little awkward at first, and you will stumble, but soon it will become completely natural.

Now we are going to put this knowledge into action and use it to counter real objections you might face. Ahead lies your objection-counter list!

We all know that feeling of coming up with the perfect comeback—the only problem being that you were insulted hours ago. You put your creative juices to work thinking up the wittiest comeback you could muster, but your time to lay that verbal smack down has come and gone. Too bad, because you know JUST what to say.

When you build an objection-counter list, you will be ready with a witty comeback to everything that comes your way. This is where you plan out the objections that could come up when you are talking to a customer, and think up the best way to counter them.

Depending on the reason you're calling, you may not have many objections. However, you should still plan for what might happen on the calls.

The most common objection you will face is the "I don't have time to talk right now" objection.

Here are a few possible ways you could counter this:
- "That is totally fine. Is there another time I can call back today when you might have some free time?"
- "I understand. This call is really out of the blue. Would you have a few minutes to answer a couple quick questions? Whenever you need to get off the phone is totally fine."
- "That's fine. Is there someone else in the office who could help me

out with _____?"

Depending on your market, there may be many different ways to counter objections. What has worked for me is to keep the counters conversational and lively. If you stay conversational and lively during the call, your prospect will warm up to you much more quickly. I've had many prospects who started out icy cold when I initially called them, only to become warm cuddly teddy bears after I handled their objections so well.

With this in mind, here a few of the objections I faced when trying to sell window cleaning services to customers (to give you an idea of how I overcame them successfully). You may think that handling window cleaning objections has nothing to do with validating business ideas, but remember the Karate Kid: Daniel didn't think that waxing cars for Mr. Miyagi had anything to do with karate, but it turned out to be pretty useful.

The objections you are going to face are the questions your prospect is likely to ask, as well as the questions you are afraid of your prospect asking. They will mostly be unique to you, your industry, and your motivation for calling.

Read these window cleaning objections to prime your mind for how to handle prospect worries while still keeping the conversation upbeat. Then I'll show you some objections that have to do with cold calling prospects in a B2B market.

Window Cleaning Objections

Are you guys safe? – Yes, all of us are extensively trained in safety. We use stabilizers and someone to hold the ladder. I would never have my employees do something that wasn't 100% safe.

You cost too much. – My prices are competitive with all other companies, and I'm so sure you won't find a better price that I give you my personal guarantee. If you ever find a competitor that is less expensive than me, I will beat THEIR price by 5%. All you have to do is show me their quote in writing when we get there to do the job and I will lower my price.

OR – There isn't anything I can do about the price, UNLESS you refer me to some of your neighbors or schedule work when we are doing the house next door. (Have options ready!)

I need to speak to my husband/wife. – That is totally fine. For now we can schedule a tentative date to secure your time in my schedule. I can give you a call later tonight or next week to confirm that it is alright with them, and then we can go from there.

I'm afraid you'll damage my stucco/eaves/wall. – I want to make sure we never do any damage to your property. If we do, there is two million dollar liability insurance. But we won't need that, because I am going to use ladder stabilizers in order to not dent your wall. And if you want us to be extra safe, I can wrap rags around the stabilizers to cushion it even further. It is my goal you leave your house in better condition than when I found it.

What if you do a bad job? – I cannot promise that every job will be perfect, but I can promise this: You do not pay until you are 100% satisfied. If you notice any streaks on windows or anything, call me up and I will personally come by and fix whatever is troubling you. Your satisfaction is my priority.

I can't commit to a day right now. – I totally understand. Planning a day to get work done is nearly impossible since you don't know what your schedule will look like then. I see you had work done around May 12th. Do you normally get work done around that time? (Yes.) Then what we can do is set up a tentative date for May 12th, and what I'll do is call you a week before that day, as well as send you reminder emails. If you want to cancel or reschedule at a later date, that's totally fine. This is just so I know around how many people are in my schedule. How does May 12th tentatively sound to you?

I use another company. – That is totally fine. But to see if you are getting the best value for your dollar, how about I do a competitive quote? At the very least you will know if they are charging you a fair rate for their work.

OR – I would really like to do this work for you. Is there anything I could do for you that would help you consider allowing me to help you out this summer?

Now, young grasshopper, you are ready to look at the business calls objection list.

Objections to Business Calls

"I don't have the money to pay for software." I can appreciate that you want to keep costs low, but think of it this way: If a software solution could stop you from losing two customers a month, then it would be more than worth the cost to you, right?

"I don't have time to talk right now." I understand, and respect your time. I think that I have a lot of value I can offer you in a call like this, either from the interesting tricks I've learned from other dentists or the software I'm eventually going to create. I would really like to get your feedback on an idea. Do you think we can schedule a time to do this call when you'll be less busy?

"I don't want to buy anything." That is totally fine. I don't want to sell you anything! Even if you're not in the market right now, I'd still love to hear about your business and see if you are facing the same challenges other dentists are facing. Your feedback could end up helping a lot of other people in your industry.

— — — — — — — — —

Exercise 4.6

Now that you have an idea of how objections and counters look, create your own. Keep it fun, and make it as close to your regular way of speaking as possible. Put down anything you are afraid of hearing on a phone call, and plan out how you can explain it away.

As with the hierarchy, when you are creating this, don't worry about being perfect—because it never will be. Just take your best guess at what objections you might face and how you are going to handle them. When you actually put your counters to the test is the only time you will really know how they hold up.

— — — — — — — — —

When you are actually doing the calling, you will get objections you hadn't thought of before—so add them to the list. If one of your objection counters isn't working, then try something else. Cold Call Karate is a process that evolves over time to better serve you.

You now have all the pieces of your call formula. In the next section I will have the complete Cold Call Battle Plan laid out in the proper order.

Your Cold Call Battle Plan

NOW THAT YOU have all the pieces of your call formula created, we are going to put that puzzle all together to create your full Cold Call Battle Plan. Below is an example of a completed call formula for someone trying to validate their dental software idea. You should have all of the pieces created already—just put it all together!

This model is laid out logically in the order that you will likely need most of the sections. If you want an editable copy of this information, you can go to growanempire.com/resources to access the extra resources associated with this book.

This is a Cold Call Battle Plan for Ryan, who has a software idea he wants to sell to dentists. He knows that slippage is a big problem for dentists, so that will be the main feature of his product. He is also still trying to figure out what other features dental offices would need from this software. Ryan wants to speak to as many dental offices as possible in order to find out if people will buy his idea.

Basic Calling Script Gatekeeper

Remember, sound agitated when on the phone with gatekeepers.
Put you through to target:

"Hey, could you put me through to (dentist's first name)?"

Put you through to someone equivalent:

"That's alright if (main dentist) is busy. Are there any other dentists around that I could have a quick word with?"

Call back at set time:

"Is there a better time I could call back when (main dentist) will be in the office?"

Email:

"Is there an email I can reach (main dentist) at?"

Voicemail:

"Could you put me through to his voicemail?"

Then say this in the voicemail:

"Hi, my name is Ryan. I'm in a software development program and I'm looking to develop software to help dentists with challenges they face on a regular basis, specifically with regards to client slippage. I'm still doing research on what kind of features dental practices would need in this software. I'd love to get your feedback on the idea. When you get a chance, call me back at 555-555-5555. Hope to speak to you soon."

Leave a message with gatekeeper:

"Could you leave (dentist's name) this message?"

Then say this:

"My name is Ryan. I'm in a software development program and I'm looking to develop software to help dentists with challenges they face on a regular basis, specifically with regards to client slippage. I'm still doing research on what kind of features dental practices would need in this software. I'd love to get (dentist's name's) feedback on the idea. When he gets a chance, tell him call me back at 555-555-5555. Hope to speak to him soon."

Pitching your Prospect
Regular pitch:

"Hi, my name is Ryan. I'm in a software development program and I'm looking to develop software to help dentists with challenges they face on a regular basis, specifically with regards to client slippage. I'm still doing research on what kind of features dental practices would need in this software. I'd love to get your feedback on the idea. It'll only take a couple of minutes."

If they offer compliance—"OK, let's do it"—then you deliver your elevator pitch.

If they have an objection—e.g., "I'm not sure I have time"—counter the objection. If they comply with that, go to the elevator pitch.

Quick pitches:

"Hi [name]. Are you interested in an easy way to make sure none of your clients slip through the cracks?"

"Hi [name]. This is Ryan. I'm calling to see if you're interested in finding an easier way to retain your clients through software."

"Are you interested in a fast and simple way to generate referrals and repeat business from your current dental clients?"

Common responses to quick pitches:

"**Sounds interesting, what is it about?**" – Go into elevator pitch.

"**Who are you and why are you calling?**" – Say "Let me just quickly explain myself." Then go into regular pitch.

They have an objection. – Counter, and then go into elevator pitch.

Elevator pitch:

"It's a software solution that will help you stay in touch with your current contact list. It helps you stay on people's minds and builds your reputation as their trusted dentist. The software service will keep track of clients that miss appointments, send them automated messages and alert your secretary to try and get in touch with them at regular intervals. I think it will really help save multiple clients each month, and keep your customers up to date on their appointments. Does it sound like something you might have use for in your business?"

Your Prospect Hierarchy

Interview on current software ideas:

"I'm looking for feedback on some of the aspects of my software. Do you mind if I run some of them by you and you can give me your feedback on it?"

Probing Questions:
- How much do you currently pay for software each month/year?
- How much is each new customer worth to you?
- Do you ever have problems with clients missing appointments? How often?
- Is there a solution you've been looking for but haven't been able to find?

Sell product/sign up for trial:

"From what I've told you about this product, if it did everything I talked about, would this be something you'd be interested in using in your dental office?"

Scheduled interview on current software ideas:

"I totally understand that you're busy right now. Is there a time this week when I could give you a call back so I cold run a few ideas by you? I want to make sure my software is a huge help to dentists."

In-person Meet-up:

"Thanks for all the feedback you've given me. You sound very knowledgeable about the industry. Is there any way that we could meet up sometime this week or the next, or I could swing by your office so I could learn more about the industry?"

Schedule virtual product demo:

"Would you be free sometime this week so I could walk you through the planned features of our software and get your feedback on it? I could share my computer screen with you so you can take a look at my plan for it. It would only take a few minutes. I think your feedback will be really useful in helping me create something dentists actually need."

Referral:

"Thanks for all the feedback you've given me. I'm trying to speak to as many dentists as possible to make an awesome product. Do you know any other dentists off the top of your head that you could recommend to have the same kind of conversation with?"

Email subscription:

"I'd like to keep in touch with all of the dentists that I'm speaking with. Do you mind if I grab your email to send you a weekly update on the development of my software?"

Schedule a follow-up call:

"Hey [first name], thanks for taking the time to talk to me. I know you're really busy. Would you be open to me giving you a call back in a few weeks to pick your brain a little bit more (or get more feedback on my project as it develops)?"

Undefined call-back time:

"Would you be open to me calling back later in the year to check in and see if you might be interested in this project as it develops more?"

Objections and Counters

"I don't have much time right now."

Just so you know, this call is on your schedule. It should only take 15 minutes. If, at any point, you need to run off and do something else, just let me know. I take no offence. Are you alright to have a quick conversation now or do you want me to call back tomorrow?

"Who are you?"

I have years of experience coding and am good friends with a dental secretary. He mentioned some of the business problems he was facing and I wanted to help. Right now I'm researching a bunch of possible problems I can solve in the dental industry. This is just a call to explore your business and see if the solution I've been working on might be right for you.

"What are you going to do with the information?"

Exactly how I use the information will depend on what we find out in this call. It could be as simple as a follow-up email with some resources, an introduction to someone else, or a full-blown product. My intention is to help you build your business in whatever way I can. This call is about finding not only the 'what,' but also the 'how.'

"This is such a strange approach."

I agree. This is definitely a strange way to research a business idea.

But I want to learn as much as possible from dentists like you. My intention is to help you find the thing that will make the biggest positive impact on your business. Maybe it will be through some resources I point you to, or maybe it will be an eventual product I create for dentists.

"**I don't have the money to pay for software.**" I can appreciate that you want to keep costs low, but think of it this way: If a software solution could stop you from losing two customers per month, then it would be more than worth the cost to you, right?

"**I don't have time to talk right now.**" I understand, and respect your time. I think that I have a lot of value I can offer you in a call like this, either from the interesting tricks I've learned from other dentists or the software I'm going to eventually create. I would really like to get your feedback on an idea. Do you think we can schedule a time to do this call when you'll be less busy?

"**I don't want to buy anything.**" That is totally fine. I don't want to sell you anything! Even if you're not in the market right now, I'd still love to hear about your business and see if you are facing the same challenges other dentists are facing. Your feedback could end up helping a lot of other people in your industry.

Exercise 4.7

Arrange all the pieces of the Cold Call Battle Plan you have created in previous chapters so they resemble a document like this. This is your sacred scripture, forged by your own two hands. It will guide you in your cold calling endeavours. As I have said many times before, use my work as a guide, but make the script your own.

And that's it! If you have this document ready, you will be totally prepared (maybe even over-prepared) to start actually doing the calls. I'm going to be walking you through, step by step, to get you calling your clients.

CHAPTER Five:
Doing the Calls

Ryan Mulvihill

THE GRASSHOPPER IS READY

YOU ARE READY, young grasshopper, to start making the calls. If you have followed all the steps I have laid out in this book, then I would even say you are over-prepared. Even so, you probably feel like there is so much more research you have to do before making the calls. You may be thinking things like:

- I need to learn about sales before I start calling. I better watch that eight-hour sales seminar on YouTube. Then I'll finally be ready to call.
- I better practice more so I don't burn through any of my leads. Always be prepared, I always say!
- I just realized that cold calling will not work for my business, at least not right now. I'll start this process later.

Notice a common theme between all of these excuses? They are preventing you from taking action right now. You'll always be more prepared later—that is the main excuse to not take action now. The thing is, when you are actually doing the calls, you will learn at breakneck speed. You will quickly realize what areas you are weak in and need to work on, and then improve.

Your only real excuse for not starting right now is that you're scared. And if you really feel scared, then read through the fears section again. Right now. Don't worry, I'll be waiting right here for you to get back.

In my time of training people, I've never had a student jump at the opportunity of doing phone calls. After my lectures, they usually say, "Ummm...can I watch you do a few phone calls first?" A reasonable request, but one that is rooted in avoidance. Most people want to do whatever they can to avoid making calls. Your brain is going to spoon feed you a few acceptable excuses as to why you shouldn't do any calling right now.

Do not trust it!

You are perfectly ready to start doing your calls right now. That doesn't necessarily mean you will be very good at it, but you have to start somewhere. Getting good will come with time, practice, and experience, so you should get started immediately.

It is time to hold yourself accountable. You know you have to do it, to at least to try it out and see the value of it yourself. Even though you know it could really help make your dream business a reality, your brain is going to make a whole lot of excuses to try and stop you from doing this. You will need some outside support, mainly in the form of an accountability partner. So your exercise, before you even start calling, is to find this person and make them an offer they can't refuse.

An accountability partner is someone who can hold you accountable to doing what you need to do. Usually it's from a one-sided bet you make with them. You might them, "I will go to the gym three times this week or I owe you $100." The accountability partner's job is to check in with you at the end of the week and ask if you kept your promise. If not, you have to pony up the cash. If you do what you said you would do, congratulations—that is a victory in itself.

Many of my clients and I have used accountability partners to help us get things done. I even used an accountability partner while writing this book. I told him, "If I don't write 500 words every day this week, I owe you $20. That's it. At the end of the week, I held to my commitment, even when I really didn't want to. There were some nights that I was really banging away at my keyboard to get my work done, but if I hadn't had that threat of losing money hanging over my head, I probably would have just gone to sleep.

One of my clients and I reached an agreement after our coaching session: 10 calls per day, or $50 is deposited to "Ryan's Party Time Charity" for every day missed. I checked in on him daily to see if I would be getting some free money, but alas, I was pleasantly disappointed every time. Unfortunately for me, my charitable cause received no donations. Fortunately for my client, it was one of his most productive prospect-calling weeks.

If you don't have a friend to give free money to, then you can check out something like stickk.com. This is the same as an accountability partner, except your money will be going to an anti-charity, aka a ridiculous charity like the George W. Bush memorial library and museum.

Exercise 5.1

Now you have to make a commitment to reaching out to your target market, and not wussing out (so to speak). Choose your accountability partner and tell them this:

"Congratulations, you are now my accountability partner. I have a goal of speaking to 20 people in my market this week. If I miss my commitment, I owe you 50$ (or 100, or 1000—whatever hurts, but won't force you to eat Ramen noodles for the next week). I'll send you an email at the end of the week confirm I hit my goal. If you don't see an email by 10pm Sunday, you can assume I missed my goal and can demand the money from me."

It's that simple. No blood pact necessary (though encouraged). Once you have uttered these words there is no going back. If you don't pick an accountability partner, I wouldn't be surprised if you drop out of the program early. Just remember that I told you so.

———————

With your accountability partner now in tow you can be confident you are going to do your calls, or face embarrassment and wallet drain. To encourage you to start calling, I'll share a few stories about my experiences training clients on the art of Cold Call Karate.

You read through the fears section and think, *Yeah, calling won't be a problem.* Then you have to actually make the calls and suddenly you feel the most unprepared you have ever been in your entire life.

You are not alone. When I was first starting to train people on cold calling into markets, it was difficult to say the least. Here are a few short stories to tell you about the pains of people trying to cold call for the first time:

Would you push the button?

I had one person who was so scared to actually do the calls that I had do reach over and press the dial button in Skype. He hemmed and hawed about needing to get his thoughts in order, despite having his entire Cold Call

Battle Plan ready to go and sitting in front of him.

He was scared to start because he was afraid of failure.

When he made a few phone calls and realized people were nice and receptive to him, he very easily overcame his fear. He had been utterly convinced that he would get a negative reaction, despite no evidence to that regard.

The lesson to be learned here is that sometimes you need someone to push the call button. Once the phone starts ringing you will figure out a way to handle it.

What if they don't like me?

Another of the people I was training was sure that people wouldn't want to talk to him. He was one of the nicest guys I've ever met, but he was convinced that he would get yelled off the phone.

The first call went through and he got to speak to a higher up in a real estate office. They were on the phone for about an hour. He learned more about his market in that short period than he did through most of his research. The realtor was happy to talk to him and offered his email address to answer further questions later.

After that amazing telephone call, Jackson became one of my most accomplished cold callers. He was completely over his fear of calling after getting that one big positive experience.

Not all of Jackson's calls went this smoothly. In fact, a few of them went horribly. But after getting some positive experiences under his belt he knew he could do it again. Often all it takes to beat your fear of calling is having one call go really well. It probably won't be your first call, but it will happen in a shorter period of time than you think. Keep trying until you get that positive experience, as it will multiply your confidence in your next calls.

The Original Terminator

Then there was Kendra. She was a sarcastic person in general, and let me know how unenthused she was to do the calling. The first few times she did some phone calls she sounded like a robot. She sounded like the Terminator as she called into boutique stores, asking what they thought of a new promotional item.

Kendra was nervous about the phone calls so she came off as rigid to the people she was calling. Normally she was quite friendly to talk to. After getting her to act completely overexcited on her phone calls. she started to gain some traction. She had to amp her excitement level up to "kid at Disney world" levels. After practicing that for a while she became more comfortable sounding excited on the phone. She became a fantastic caller for the organization I was consulting with.

To sum up all of these stories, most of my students failed, at least initially, but then learned from their mistakes and quickly got better. You will get much better, no matter what your starting level is—I can guarantee that.

The best part of this process is that you are supposed to fail, initially. You have taken your best guess as to how you will get to speak to your market, and are executing the plan. As you make calls, you will quickly realize what's working and what isn't. Then you just have to alter your strategy to adapt to this new information.

So now let's get to making those calls!

Fun With Roleplay

NOW YOU ARE finally going to start making the calls. Here is how I would lay out everything to give you the best chances for success.

Taking notes

Get a notebook to take down mid-call notes. Clanking away on a keyboard will throw off your prospect, so I believe that a notebook is a much better tool to take notes. Use it to write down things that you want to ask follow-up questions about in your calls. You don't need to write down every thing your prospect says, just important stuff you want to follow up on during the conversation. Detailed notes can wait until you have finished the call and take a listen to the recording.

Keep track of everything

I would suggest keeping all your contacts open in an Excel spreadsheet so you can write down notes after the call. Many people think they can keep track of all their prospects in their heads, but I'm sorry to say they are wrong. You need to keep track of prospect notes from when you start calling for the first time or you are going to forget who said what, who you already called, and who not to call again.

After your calls, you can type into the notes section of your Excel spreadsheet so you know the main points to follow up on in your future communications. Having a section to write down tasks associated with prospects will be very useful, as you don't want to forget to email them that information you promised them. Lastly, color-coding the spreadsheet will make your life much easier when calling through the list multiple times.

Have your scripts ready

Have your Cold Call Battle Plan printed out, in front of you, for easy access. That way you have to do as little thinking as possible when you are on the calls. You aren't going to be following your process exactly during every call, but if you don't have it in front of you, then you will forget many of the things you hoped to talk about.

I can't tell you how many times people forgot to ask for a referral or an email address after a positive call because they didn't look at their Call Formulas. If they had just glanced at their scripts, they wouldn't have missed a golden opportunity to get some easy leads. Don't miss opportunities. Glance back at your Call Formula once in a while to make sure you don't forget to ask certain questions.

Record your calls

Have your call recorder running on your computer or phone at all times. I make all my calls through Skype, and use MP3 Skype Recorder. It automatically records all your Skype calls and conveniently names the files so it's easy to find them again. This lets you not have to worry about missing something that your contact says, so you can focus on the conversation at hand. You can download it here: voipcallrecording.com/

MP3_Skype_Recorder

I highly recommend getting an automated call recorder. I had a Skype recorder once where I had to click record at the start of every call. I forgot to click it. Every. Single. Time. Also, having a recorder that automatically names the files is a godsend, as you can quickly look up your recordings later when you are in review mode.

Commit to a time

Commit to a time to make your calls during business hours. Block off one- to three-hour time slots in your schedule to do your calls. Make sure you tell your accountability partner when you plan to be making these calls so they can keep on top of you. Stick to a schedule, and plan to try out Cold Call Karate for at least two weeks to see if it's right for your business.

Pro tip: If you live on the east coast and work nine to five, then you can still call into the west coast after 5pm EST, because of time zones!

That's all the logistics you need to start making your calls. Now, to make you over-prepared to start calling, I'm going to get you to have some fun with role-playing.

— — — — — — — — — —

Exercise 5.2

Role-play through your Cold Call Battle Plan. Get one of your friends to sit down with you and pretend to be a prospect in your market. Tell them a little about the market so they can play the part, then run through your entire Cold Call Battle Plan with them. This will get you used to how conversations will flow. Don't have them follow the script word for word. Try to get them to throw you a bit of a curve ball once in a while.

To get a proper role-playing experience, make sure you pretend like your friend is actually your prospect. Take notes, voice record the role-play, and make fake notes on your Excel spreadsheet. You want to get as real of a feel as possible for what it will really be like when you start making your calls. That way, it will feel natural when you actually start doing the calls.

After you have run through the script a few times, it's time for the big leagues.

It is that time. We are finally going to make some calls!

COLD CALL TIME

THAT'S ALL YOU really need set up to do your calls. And of course a hypothetical set of brass balls. (I'm not above making *Glengarry Glen Ross* references.) If you have done everything I have laid out above, then you can start making your calls ASAP. Just dive right into your learning, and expect to learn from all the mistakes you are going to make.

No matter how underprepared you feel for your calls, I can guarantee you are as prepared as you are ever going to be. Don't let doubt sneak into your mind. Let's get these calls done!

To make this even easier for you I have created a workbook called "Your First 20 Calls". This has a list of questions and evaluation to fill out while doing these first 20 calls. It will force you to evaluate how the call went and what you can do to improve the next call. It can be found at Growanempire.com/resources.

— — — — — — — — —

Exercise 5.3

It is the moment you have been eagerly waiting for—time to make those calls.

- Get your Excel spreadsheet ready with all of your leads. (If you don't

have one ready, then do a Google search and find a couple phone numbers from your target market to use in the meantime. Don't worry about emailing these people for now.)
- If you do have a leads list ready, then send out your pre-heater email blast (if you haven't already).
- Set aside three hours in your schedule to make the calls, and commit to this time.
- Get your accountability partner and set your terms, including when you'll have the calls done by.
- Print out your Cold Call Battle Plan.
- Get your notebook and pen ready.
- Get your call recorder set up.
- Sit down at your allotted time and dial. It's that simple.
- Test out your call formula on 20 people (Getting rejected still counts towards this goal, as long as you managed to speak to your prospect). "No answers" don't count towards this goal, and neither do calls if the gatekeeper tells you that your prospect isn't in the office. You have to try your pitch and either get rejected or accepted 20 times, minimum.
- Have your first 20 calls workbook ready to fill out after each call. Remember only fill it out when you try to pitch your prospect and speak to them for a few minutes.

— — — — — — — — —

Speak to 20 people before you move on to the next section. I want you to truly understand what cold calling is before we try to improve your technique. Only after you talk to at least 20 people and review some of your call recordings will you understand the post-calls section.

The Pep Talk You Need

DID YOU MAKE your calls?

Here we are. You made it to the section where you can take real action to turn your business idea into a reality. But are you going to?

Do you find yourself constantly TELLING people about your business ideas, only to find months later that you haven't made any progress? Sitting in an office staring at the clock until five starts to look like a viable option. But you know where the nine to five path leads, and you don't want to be a part of it. You have a choice to make right now. Are you going to actually take action on your business idea? Or are you just going to spend your time talking to people about it?

Maybe you get a nice logo designed. Sketch up some ideas. But when it comes to actually finding customers and trying to make money with your idea, you freeze. You hesitate. Before you take this action, your business is just a fantasy for you to play with in your mind. You can postulate about how great it could be when you finally get around to it. But you never do.

There's an easy split between the two types of entrepreneurial people I know—there's the talkers and the doers. The talkers will spend all their time telling you about their amazing idea.

Startup Idea Action Plan

I was a talker once. We all were. Now what I want you to do is to graduate from that stage. It's time to take the real action that will turn your business into a reality.

Congratulations on making it this far in the book. But I have to tell you, this knowledge is both a blessing and a curse.

You are blessed by knowing a simple system that can be applied to almost any business idea, and can start taking the right action on it immediately.

But it's also a curse because it removes your excuses. You can no longer tell yourself you just don't know how to move your business forward. You know a fantastic way to get it done. From this point on, if you don't take action on your business ideas, you may have to accept that you aren't destined to be an entrepreneur. Maybe you are destined to sit in an office cubicle your whole life, your soul slowly being vacuumed out of you in exchange for meagre pay. Reading all these books on entrepreneurship is ultimately a waste of time, as you aren't going to do anything with the knowledge anyway. You may as well put down the book, pucker your lips, and prepare to ass kiss your way up the corporate ladder. By the end of it you'll have a nice company Rolex watch and a pat on the back telling you what a valued employee you've been.

I've seen this happen to many people close to me, except they didn't even get the luxury of a watch or a pat on the back. This isn't a far-fetched story, this is the reality that faces many people close to you right now. And it could very well be your life story—if you let it.

I'm giving you a choice right now—to pursue your business idea and take action, or let it fall by the wayside, as you have before. What are you going to do about it?

Some people are still scared to take action and need that extra push of having a coach. It is 100% possible to do this process all by yourself, but if you need a push, I do offer coaching. You can check it out at growanempire.com/coaching.

I'm going to give you one last chance to go back through this book and do the exercises (if you've skipped them). But without taking action, this book has just been a whole lot of mental masturbation.

What this book is doing is offering you a chance to realize your potential. This is your path off of your plateau to start climbing to new heights.

A year from now, do you want to look back to today and think, *I can't believe how far I've come*, OR are you going to look back and say, "Nothing has really changed?"

Are you ready to take action?
Make those calls.

Chapter Six:
After The Calls

Ryan Mulvihill

You Did It!

CONGRATULATIONS ON DOING your calls—it takes a lot of guts to go through with it. Many people would much rather fantasize about getting work done then actually doing it. You were probably shocked by how your conversations went. A lot of people are very skeptical when I tell them that talking to their market is as simple as picking up the phone and calling. They have negative assumptions about how people will react to receiving a phone call from them. People are usually very friendly and open to having a conversation with you about your business idea. Even the ones who don't want to talk to you are mostly exceedingly polite about it.

A big mindset shift I had after doing a ton of these calls was realizing that I am actually adding excitement to people's lives by giving them a call. Most people's days blend together when working for a business, with every day being similar to the next. But then one day they receive a phone call from a spunky entrepreneur with ideas for making a business. It brings them out of their regular routine to look into an interesting new idea that could improve their lives. They should be thanking you for calling them.

As for the calls that you did, take a look at these metrics to help gauge your success:

- About 1 in 10 people you call will speak to you.
- About 1 in 3 of those will have a long conversation with you.
- A call goes well if it lasts 10 minutes.
- A call that goes really well will last 30 minutes or more.
- For about every hour of calling you do you'll get 1–2 conversations that go well.

These factors can vary depending on your niche. The more comfortable you get with calling, the more often you will get conversations that go well.

After you have made your 20 calls and listen to yourself speak, you are going to realize that things didn't go perfectly. You probably cringed at how you sounded on the phone. Have no fear—Ryan will fix you! It won't be easy, though. This is the hardest part of the process to teach. It is the most abstract and indefinable step in the process that I've laid out. It is the tone of your voice and how confident you appear over the phone.

— — — — — — — — —

Exercise 6.1

I want you to listen to the recordings of your calls. Listen to a few of the ones that went well, and a few of the ones that didn't go well. Listen for how you sounded in the calls, and answer these questions for each of the recordings you listen to.

What went well during this call?
What went badly during this call?
What can I do better?
How did I sound during the call?

This should be done in addition to your first 20 calls workbook. The insights you get from listening to your call recordings will be invaluable

You won't need an in-depth analysis of each of your phone calls. You will hear where you need to improve and where you are dropping the ball. When you know what went well during a phone call, you can focus on emphasizing those positive points during your next calls. When you know what you really need to improve on in your calls, you can fix those areas. Just having a general idea of where you need to improve during your phone calls will help you immensely during your next calls.

This process of reviewing your calls will refine your call script. Maybe people aren't responding very well to some of your lead-in questions, so you change it up. Maybe there is a particular objection that you have faced a few times that you need to beat. Find your areas you are weak in and refine your process to bolster them.

I can't give advice to every unique situation, so here is where you need to use your best judgment in order to make your process better.

The best advice I can give you for refining your call process is to listen to the calls that went well and find the commonalities between them. Maybe bringing up a certain question in your call script made conversations flow a lot more smoothly. Maybe taking a more friendly, energized tone of voice made your prospect much easier to talk to. Look for these commonalities and emphasize them in your calls going forward.

That last question I have on the list may sound a little weird, but how you speak is the BIGGEST factor in whether someone will actually listen to you. You could have your entire sales process ready and know exactly how you are going to talk to a client, but because your voice sounds shaky they will want to get off the phone as soon as possible. If you sound a little strange on the phone, don't worry—you are not alone. When you have answered the questions, read the stories below of people who were once newbies just like you.

———————

You probably found a bunch of areas you can improve on after your calls. In addition to improving your script, you will need to improve your tone of voice. After listening to your call recordings you will probably find you are suffering from one of these four ailments. They have to do with the way you speak when you are a little nervous. I've given each of them names to for my own amusement, and to try and work more alliteration into my literature.

- Speedy Freddy
- Scared Jared
- Terminator Tom
- Bully Hoodie

Let's look at each of these in detail and figure out how we can overcome them.

Speedy Freddy

Speedy Freddy talks at breakneck speed. He talks so fast that the person he's talking to doesn't even get a chance to join in the conversation. Freddy is so focused on what he wants to say that he doesn't leave room for the other side of the conversation to throw him off. If the prospect seems unenthusiastic about continuing the conversation, Freddy panics and talks even faster. Freddy hears the sound of being hung up on more than actually hearing someone say bye to him.

One woman I was coaching was a pretty fast talker to begin with, and when she was nervous her vocal pace went supersonic. She would often talk prospects off the phone, and they would hang up out of frustration. The best way I found to help her out was to sit next to her on her calls and lower my hand in a "slow down" motion when she was speeding up too much. She started to notice when she was starting to go too fast, and began to self-regulate. Soon she was slowing down enough to handle all her calls, no problem.

If you are a Speedy Freddy, the cure is to slow things down (obviously). Less is really more when it comes to these sort of conversations. You want to try and get the other person to engage with you, and talking AT them will just drive them away. Try to shift your attention to listening to what they have to say, and give a two-second pause to make sure they are finished with their thought.

When you listen to a recording of yourself, it will be pretty cringe-worthy. That's ok if you talk a little fast. You will fix it pretty easily with some outside help. For this problem, I'd suggest having one of your friends sit next to you and signal when you're talking too fast. You won't really notice it yourself at first, so having an extra pair of eyes watching you will be immensely useful. Eventually, as you become more comfortable with your phone speak, you will slow down.

Scared Jared

Scared Jared is terrified of talking on the phone. To his prospect he sounds like the mafia is holding him hostage and forcing him to make calls to pay back his debts. Some people—usually the ones with social anxiety—are faced with this mental block. The act of talking to someone you don't know scares you so much your voice trembles. It happens because you are terrified of the person on the other end of the line.

One person I was coaching sounded so scared during his phone calls that he weirded out most of his prospects. When he spoke to one lady, she agreed to answer a few of his questions. His response was a long pause, and asking, "Are you sure?" The lady on the other end of the phone now felt awkward. "Sorry, there's actually something I have to do," she said as she hung up the phone. I was flabbergasted that my student could drop the ball like that. But when you're first learning this skill you likely won't notice even the most elementary mistakes.

Odds are you aren't scared to talk to your friends over the phone, so you have to trick yourself into thinking you are talking to a good friend. We will be doing this with role-play to warm you up to the idea of talking to strangers. Have a friend, loved one, or confidante sit next to you and role-play phone calls with you. Have them pretend to be one of your prospects as you run through your Cold Call Battle Plan. By getting used to talking to a friend in this context you will start talking to prospects like they are your friends, which will make you less scared-sounding on the phone.

When you try talk to prospects like your friends, it takes the pressure off of you to regulate your speech. You are free to make jokes and come off a little awkward sometimes. It's this pressure you are putting on yourself to preform that is tripping you up. You need to get loose. Chill out, bro. You'll desensitize yourself to the calls after having many practice phone calls with your friends. When you start doing the real calls again, you should keep a friend by your side to give you moral support (and laugh at the hilarious rejections, of course). Anything that takes the pressure off will aid your calls immensely.

Terminator Tom

Terminator Tom is a robot sent from the future to suck the life out of every conversation. He talks completely monotone, and sounds like he's reading a script—which in a way he is. Some people are really scared when they start to learn how to cold call, so they stick right to their script. And when you read directly off a script it comes out as the most boring talk imaginable. People usually think you are some sort of telemarketer, just from the fact that there is no passion in your voice.

I had one woman I was training named Kendra, and she had a serious case of the terminator voice. She was fine talking to people on the phone, but her voice was just devoid of all emotion. I knew she was driving away a couple qualified leads purely from being so unexcited to do the calls. I then had a few rounds of role-play cold calling practice with her to help her with her robo-voice. I told her to pretend that this phone call was the most exciting thing in the world. She was to pretend to be overexcited to interview my boutique about a new promotional item she was considering selling. When she thought she was sounding like an overly excited schoolgirl I knew she was overcoming the robo-voice.

This is one of the more difficult ailments to cure a newbie cold caller from. In order to sound less robotic, you have to learn how to sound very excited about whatever you are talking about. Pretend that whatever you are talking about is the most exciting thing you've ever spoken about on the phone. You have to be positively ecstatic about interviewing your target market. They have to feel your enthusiasm pour out the phone and into their ear canals. This is how you set the tone of the conversation.

If you have an unexcited robo-voice when you are calling customers, then they are going to be even less enthusiastic to be talking to you. The only way to amp up a prospect's energy is to be very energetic and friendly yourself. So you may have to role-play with a friend in order to experiment with a high-energy way of talking to prospects. Try to sound almost comically excited when you first start practicing, and then tone it down from there. For most kinds of calls, sounding over-excited will get you much farther then sounding under excited.

Bully Hoodie

This usually only applies to people who have some previous sales experience. In the world of sales, sometimes being pushy can get you the sale. If you push harder, you can sometimes break through objections and sell your wares. This only works for certain types of sales, like selling cell phone contracts and possibly window cleaning services. The type of calls I'm preparing you for you are trying to create a dialog with the prospect. Sometimes, if a prospect is a little hesitant to talk to you, it is possible to bully them into having a conversation with you. But it will usually be a hollow victory.

I was training a man named Dave to do some customer interview calls. He had experience selling cell phone plans for a major carrier and was used to very pushy sales tactics. The calls were to get customer feedback on a product Dave's company was considering launching. Dave had been battle hardened by his time doing calls selling phone contracts, and would try to push through every rejection a customer had to get his way. Because of this, he could get customers who were not into a phone conversation to stay on the phone and talk to him. They would try to be polite with him, and talk to him even if they had no interest in what he was selling. Dave thought he was getting positive feedback on his products, but what he was really getting was people too polite to hang up the phone. They would give him obviously false feedback because he pushed them into saying it. He would be a fantastic police interrogator.

After he pitched a prospect the conversation would often go like this:

"...So now that I've told you about our product idea, do you think it's something you could see selling in your store?"

"*Ummm...I'm not sure if it's really for us.*"

"Alright, but do you like the idea of it?"

"*I guess it's alright.*"

"So you think that this product would be a good idea for other stores?"

"*Yeah, I guess so.*"

"Great! So you think it would sell really well in other establishments. I'm glad you really like our product. Want me to add you to our email list to reach out when we develop our product further? Maybe you'll change your mind and want to buy from us later?"

"*Yeah, that sounds good. My email is xxxxx.*"

After a conversation like this, Dave would look up at me and say, "Great! Another business owner that thinks our idea is awesome, and wants to be added to our email list!" But that customer wasn't interested—they were just being polite, and he managed to push them into sounding excited about our services.

This is a much easier ailment to cure, as it is not based in fear. If you are using pushy salesman tactics on your calls, then you need to tone it down and focus more on the conversation. It may mean that you get less feedback from customers, but it will mean better quality feedback. Better quality feedback means better information to make decisions. If you find yourself pressure selling when you are really trying to start a discussion, then you know you have to tone down your tactics.

When you first start calling your prospects, odds are you will be afflicted with one of these ailments. All of them have slightly different tactics to overcome them, but it all boils down to one simple idea—practice and you WILL get better. Cold calling will be tough, but if you have enough practice you will figure out the best way to conduct your calls.

Cold calling is a process that you get much more effective at over time. However, you will be pretty terrible at it at first. Fixing your tone is a good first step in making yourself an effective caller. Don't worry about being perfect—just know your weaknesses and actively try to improve them.

Speaking about getting better, if you want to improve, you need to take into account what you do after the phone calls. This is what will accelerate your process.

Track Your Calls

AFTER MAKING THE calls there are two things you have to keep in mind in order to be a successful caller. Keep track and review.

Keeping track usually comes in phases. At first, when you've only called around 20 people, you can keep everything in your head. You think, Yeah I can remember to follow up with these 10 people at their own specific times. Then as you call more and more people you'll eventually have a list of around 100 people packed into a single excel spreadsheet. You'll have notes on them, color coding, and sorting so you think you're keeping on top of your prospects.

In reality if you use a system like this, many prospects are going to fall through the cracks. You are going to feel utterly overwhelmed scrolling through your excel spreadsheet. I have been there a few times, and it's not fun. I had 2 different rows for color codes on a customer list I was working on in my newbie days. It was a headache that made me almost wish I was colorblind.

Now you can skip all this pain and use a CMS (Customer Management System) to keep track of things for you. I highly recommend a CMS called "Insightly". It's cheap, and will allow you to make customer files, and set tasks and reminders to follow up with people. It will make your life much easier if you start using a simple CMS like this one from the start. You can even upload your excel spreadsheet right into Insightly to easily get started.

Reviewing your calls is just as important as tracking them. You don't have to re listen to the recording of every call you make. You do however need to look for the areas you, or your script are weak in. This is your chance to experiment with the way you're calling in order to make the process better.

A big part of this process is that you need to refine your scripts based on the feedback you get from your market. Your script starts off as your best guess on how people will respond and evolves as you take your calls.

If you think a call went badly, and it was because of something you did, then listen to the recording. It will be a little cringe worthy listening to calls that went south, but how can you improve if you don't? You may quickly find you are saying "Um..." too often, or saying "like" more often then a blonde from California. Learn from your mistakes, don't beat yourself up about it.

On the same token, when a call goes really well you should re listen to it again. You can learn from your successes just as much as you can learn from your mistakes. Try and figure out what makes this caller so much more receptive towards you, and see if you can do it more in future calls. Keep track of your prospects and keep track of yourself. Cold Call Karate is a process that will develop over time. So have fun with it, and make it your own.

You made your best guess on how your target market would react to your calls. Some assumptions were right, some were wrong. Now you have to get to the real work of improving your system. If a phrase is coming off awkwardly, change it. If you think the process needs to be reworked, then go for it. Use the feedback from your market, and adapt to it, to make you stronger.

This process I have taught you is not the end of your entrepreneurial journey. I have just taught you a way to speed up and systematize answering the big question, "Will people buy my idea?". Now it's all on you to find that answer.

There are generally three possible outcomes from the Cold Call Karate process

The first is researching a market only to find that customers had no need for what you were planning to offer or are just generally unreachable. Heart surgeons are not likely to put down the scalpel to answer phone calls, unfortunately. Or fortunately, depending on if they are operating on you at the moment. If that's the case, congratulations on finding out early and not wasting very much time on an unfeasible business idea.

The next possibility is that this process proves successful. By following this process you have pulled a bunch of customers out of thin air. You very quickly learned exactly what your market finds important, leading to a better product. You manage to get a bunch of pre-orders and sell on the initial launch. You become a successful entrepreneur because you learned from your market before investing time and money into an idea.

The third, most awesome possibility is a pivot. You may find that your market isn't looking for what you wanted to offer—but you find a new pain they have that you can solve with a product. Now you have a really great idea for a product that you uncovered with researching the market. That is a huge win. You now have a business idea that customers really want.

That is the ideal I want you to strive for, successful business owner. I have only really given you the first step, but it is really more of a solid footing. There is a lot more work ahead of you to turn that business idea into a reality. After following the Cold Call Karate Process you are set up to take some big steps with your business idea. Let's talk about what you can do after completing this Cold Call Karate process.

Taking Action on Your Info

AFTER MAKING THE calls, there are two things you have to keep in mind in order to be a successful caller: Keep track and review.

Keeping track usually comes in phases. At first, when you've only called around 20 people, you can keep everything in your head. You think, *"Yeah I can remember to follow up with these 10 people at their own specific times"*. Then, as you call more and more people, you'll eventually have a list of around 100 people packed into a single Excel spreadsheet. You'll have notes on them, color-coding, and sorting, so you think you're keeping on top of your prospects.

In reality, if you use a system like this, many prospects are going to fall through the cracks. You are going to feel utterly overwhelmed scrolling through your Excel spreadsheet. I have been there a few times, and it's not fun. I had two different rows for color codes on a customer list I was working on in my newbie days. It was a headache that made me almost wish I was colorblind.

Now you can skip all this pain and use a CMS (customer management system) to keep track of things for you. I highly recommend a CMS called "Insightly." It's cheap, and will allow you to make customer files and set tasks and reminders to follow up with people. It will make your life much easier if you start using a simple CMS like this one from the start. You can even upload your Excel spreadsheet right into Insightly to easily get started.

Reviewing your calls is just as important as tracking them. You don't have to re-listen to the recording of every call you make. You do, however, need to look for the areas you or your script are weak in. This is your chance to experiment with the way you're calling in order to make the process better.

A big part of this process is that you need to refine your script based on the feedback you get from your market. Your script starts off as your best guess on how people will respond, and evolves as you take your calls.

If you think a call went badly, and it was because of something you did, then listen to the recording. It will be a little cringe-worthy listening to calls that went south, but how can you improve if you don't? You may quickly find you are saying, "Um..." too often, or saying, "Like" more often then a blonde from California. Learn from your mistakes—don't beat yourself up about them.

On the same token, when a call goes really well you should re-listen to it again. You can learn from your successes just as much as you can learn from your mistakes. Try and figure out what makes this caller so much more receptive towards you, and see if you can do it more in future calls. Keep track of your prospects and keep track of you. Cold Call Karate is a process that will develop over time, so have fun with it and make it your own.

You made your best guess on how your target market would react to your calls. Some assumptions were right, some were wrong. Now you have to get to the real work of improving your system. If a phrase is coming off awkwardly, change it. If you think the process needs to be reworked, then go for it. Use the feedback from your market, and adapt to it to make you stronger.

This process I have taught you is not the end of your entrepreneurial journey. I have just taught you a way to speed up and systematize answering the big question, "Will people buy my idea?" Now it's all on you to find that answer.

If you were researching a market, maybe you found that customers had no need for what you were planning to offer, or were just generally unreachable. Heart surgeons are not likely to put down the scalpel to answer phone calls, unfortunately. Or fortunately, depending on if they are operating on you at the moment. If that's the case, congratulations on finding out early and not wasting very much time on an unfeasible business idea.

The other possibility is that this process proves successful. By following this process you have pulled a bunch of customers out of thin air. You very quickly learned exactly what your market finds important, leading to a better product. You manage to get a bunch of pre-orders and sell on the initial launch. You become a successful entrepreneur because you learned from your market before investing time and money into an idea.

That is the ideal I want you to strive for: successful business owner. I have only really given you the first step, but it is really more of a solid footing. There is a lot more work ahead of you to turn that business idea into a reality. After following the Cold Call Karate process you are set up to take some big steps with your business idea.

Building Your Case

SO YOU THINK your business idea is going to bring you in some money?

I want you to prove it to me.

Before you start investing large amounts of time into your business or startup idea you need to prove that people really want to buy it. Good thing this is what you have been doing throughout the whole Cold Call Karate process. Every conversation you have had with a prospect has been giving you the evidence you need to prove that there is a need in the market for what you want to sell.

You need to be able to answer these questions confidently before you can consider your idea valid:

- What is the pain you are solving with your product?
- How many people have said they are willing to pay for your product?
- How much are they willing to pay for your idea?
- How many people have you gathered on an email list that want updates on your business idea's progress?
- Roughly what percentage of the people you've talked to have been interested in your product?

Every assumption you have about your market you need to back up with proof in the form of what customers have said to you. There is no room for maybes. If you have a new thing you need to learn about the market then work it into your interview questions and Cold Call Battle Plan. You are building a case to prove your business will be successful, get on it!

— — — — — — — — — —

Exercise 6.3

As you are following the cold call karate process you need to be compiling what I call "The Proof". That is all the evidence that your business idea is going to be a success.

- Every recording you make that goes well
- Every piece of insight you learn from your market
- Everything you learn going through the Cold Call Karate process

Never worry about packing too much information into your proof folder, you can sort through it later. This is an ongoing process, as you are going through your calls and talking to your market you will be gathering your proof. Whether it is digital information like a call recording, or physical notes from when you were doing your calls, you need to know where every bit of information is.

As you go through the Cold Call Karate process continue to build up The Proof until you feel you have indisputable evidence that your business idea is going to be a success. This process could be short, or long depending on your market.

When you do feel you have indisputable evidence your business idea will be a success you are going to do some more roleplaying. Sit a friend down and have them grill you on your business idea. Have them role-play an investor who is considering putting money in your project. Your job is to use your proof to convince them to give you their investment money. Imagine you're on the show Dragons Den, and the hosts are staring you down. Will you be able to get them to invest in your business idea?

— — — — — — — — —

What will you use this proof for?

When you need to look for investors or business partners and they question whether your business idea is going to work, you will show them the proof. You may need to organize it before you start showing it to people, but you will be able to prove your business idea will be a success. On the other hand, there is a possibility you will prove the opposite. Through struggling to gather evidence for your business idea you may find proof that it is destined for failure. Let's look at this possibility…

WHAT IF MY IDEA FAILS?

IT IS DEFINITELY a possibility. The results can come back negative for your startup idea. Maybe it sounded like an awesome idea when you were first conceptualizing it, but after speaking to many people in the market you realized they don't have any need for it.

I can't really give you a solid metric to track if your business idea should be deemed a failure. It is more of a gut feeling you will get after talking to enough people in the industry. If you find it difficult to get anyone excited about your business idea, then it may be a sign to stop pursuing that particular business idea and start researching the next one.

I'll give you a real example of this happening.

I was doing consulting for a small business that would find suppliers of products in China and sell them to the Western markets. They had an idea for a folding table hook that fashion boutiques could use as a promotional item. It was a sort of a trinket item, but if they found stores that wanted to give these away in large quantities, they could make a decent recurring profit from it.

I got a leads list together for independent fashion boutiques and emailed the list. I created the Cold Call Battle Plan and trained their employees to call into the market to find out if the store owners would actually want a product like this. We started calling and researching the market eagerly.

The results came back negative. A very low percentage of the people we contacted were even slightly interested. They called it tacky, and said they wouldn't pay much for it. After calling into the market for over a week with the team of callers we decided to stop the calls. Time of death, 2:37pm on a Tuesday.

Many people would say this was a failure since the company didn't end up with a product they could sell. I actually call this a win. We found out very quickly that this idea was not going to work in the market, before the business invested significant money or time into this idea. The business owner even thanked me after I presented the findings from our calls telling him not to pursue the idea. He was relieved he didn't order a shipment of the products and build a fancy website for it.

Best of all, his team was now trained up on this Cold Call Karate process, so we were able to start research into his next idea almost immediately.

I want you to relate this story to your own endeavours, as there is a chance your idea will fail. I don't want you to be sad if this happens, I want you to be happy you found out early. Many people spend years of their lives and large chunks of their money on ideas that were never going to work. You have avoided this, for the most part. You have gotten a pretty clear idea almost immediately as to how your market will receive your idea, and if they even have a need for it. If you found out they don't want your idea, then you are poised to start looking into your next business idea almost immediately.

If your business idea fails to get much love from your prospects, then consider yourself lucky. It would be better if you found your idea to be in high demand, of course. However, learning early on that your business idea is a dud will save you time and energy you can invest in a winning business idea. You will eventually find a winner—you may just have to sort through a couple ideas first.

Keep going through the process until you find that idea that both you and your market likes. Try enough times and you will find that amazing idea. I guarantee it. And when you do find that idea, you can start to consider preselling it.

PRE-SELLING

THERE'S ALSO THE other possibility when gathering your proof. The results come out positive that your business idea is needed in the market. If so you are going to probably need some money to invest in your business idea. Wouldn't it be awesome if people paid for your product BEFORE you delivered it?

Well I'm here to tell you it IS possible.

You need to try preselling as it is the ultimate way to find out if customers are going to buy your product, by asking them to buy your product. Pretty simple eh? Not quite—to properly presell your product you need to have a few things in order.

A clear idea of what you are creating
After talking to many people in your target market you should now have a very clear idea of what sort of product they want you to create. You need to be able to concisely explain exactly what the end result of your business idea will be to your prospective customers. If it is a physical product you should have some mockup sketches of what it will look like. If it is a

software product, you need to have an outline of the UX design as well as the different features. If it is a service you will be providing you better know exactly what the service entails. Unless you can picture with crystal clarity in your mind what your end product will look like, you won't be able to presell it.

A timeline for when it will be done

Realistically how long will it take to make your business a reality? You need to know this for when you start talking to customers and preselling them. It will probably be the first question on their minds, so you better have a well thought out answer to their question.

A plan for where the money will go

The act of preselling isn't to line your pockets with cash, but rather to help fund the development of your business idea. Likely you will need to hire a coder, get some prototypes, or buy some equipment in order to turn your business idea into a reality. You need to be able to explain this to your potential customers. If you know it will cost you $3000 to buy your first batch of widgets, you better be able to present them with a spreadsheet of your estimated costs.

A professional look

If you want to convince people to give you money you need to have some sort of website set up to give yourself the look of credibility. Landing pages are very easy to throw together using a service like Squarespace or Unbounce and will allow you to build a site without having any web design knowledge. Even if it's just you working on this startup you need to really make it look like you are a professional operation. Having a nice landing page and changing your voicemail to a professional sounding one could be enough.

A new sales script

Surprise! You actually need to know how to sell your product. The good news is that after going through the Cold Call Karate process you will have a very good idea of how to do that. You will have talked to dozens of people in the market on your business ideas. You will know how to describe the pains they face on a regular basis—and how your startup is going to solve for them.

A powerful relationship with your prospect

Since your only contact with most of your potential customers has been online or over the phone they don't know you too well. You need to do everything in your power to build a relationship with the people most interested in your startup idea. Add them on social media, send them links to resources that could help their business, give them a weekly update on the progress of your business idea. You need to be touching base with them on a regular basis if they are going to have confidence in your abilities to create your business idea. If they are going to prepay for your business idea you need to make them feel as involved as possible in its creation.

An offer they can't refuse

Why should people be willing to pay for a product het isn't even ready yet. Will you be offering them 50% off the end price when you launch your product? If your product will be subscription based can you give them a free lifetime membership if they prepay for it? What can you offer to your prospects to entice them to prepay for your startup idea? You also have to be clear on the fact that they will get their money back if you fail to deliver.

— — — — — — — — —

Exercise 6.3

This is the first exercise I'm going to tell you NOT to do immediately. You should only start planning for your preselling after you spoken to many people in your market and you can prove that yes, this business idea is viable. This is what you are going to do after you have the proof your product will be successful. This is for after you have written up a business plan, and after you have a clear idea of what your business is going to look like. I want to give you an idea of what you will be doing when you are done fleshing out your business idea. You need to do some preparation in order to start selling your product, based on what I have laid out above.

- Figure out an estimate on what your business expenses are going to be in order to turn this business idea into a reality. Put them all into a spreadsheet to that you can show to prospects.
- Figure out your timeline for how long it will take to turn this business into a reality
- Figure out a clear idea of what you are going to create and what the end product will look like. Create any sketches and mockups you can show to prospects so they know what you are selling.
- Use these mockups to create a web page with the purpose of explaining your product, what it's benefits are and why they should pay for it before it is even created.

- Create a sales script to convince a prospect to buy your product.
    - Explain the benefits of your product
    - Tell why you are preselling your product and what you plan to use the money for
    - Give them an incentive to buy your product early
    - Explain you will give them their money back if you fail to deliver
    - Tell them how much you are preselling your product for

Unfortunately for this process I can't give you a step by step guide for how to package your presales to be appealing to customers. It will vary greatly depending on your relationship with the prospect, how much money you need and what you are going to sell. I can only give you the general outline so you can build it yourself when you are ready.

— — — — — — — — —

Through building up this content for the presell you are going to get yourself ready to actually start selling to prospective customers. When the time comes I highly recommend looking into the book *Spin Selling* to give you some ideas of properly pitching potential customers.

Keep in mind this is further down the road when you have a validated business idea. So don't worry about preselling your idea—just know this is the end goal of a successful business idea. I can only give you a great start on the path to creating an awesome business, I don't have all the answers.

THIS IS WHERE I LEAVE YOU

THIS IS THE conclusion of the Cold Call Karate process.

Now, when you have a business idea, you know the first step to making it a success. You have a clear path to finding your first customers and learning exactly what they would want out of your product.

This process doesn't guarantee your success—it is just stacking the cards in your favor so you have the best chances for success. If you choose to pursue a business idea, you are off to a great start, with potential customers and the confidence to speak to them. Even if your first idea turns out to be a dud, it is only a matter of time until you find that idea that is going to make you a lot of money.

Actually executing the business is not something I can teach you in the scope of this book. Depending on what type of business you are choosing to pursue there are too many variables to walk you through the startup process. However after you have your list of customers that want to buy you can confidently start investing your time and money into your business idea. When you know exactly what your customers want, it eliminates the indecisiveness that plagues most startup owners.

This isn't a complete business creation system—it's just the first step. As you build your dream business you will need to look into other resources to guide you along the way. I recommend reading *The Lean Startup* by Eric Reis, as it will give you a more complete philosophy for building a successful business. A lot of *The Lean Startup* principals helped me with creating this process. I know as you move your business idea forward *The Lean Startup* principals will help guide you to making your idea a success.

Now that you have learned this process, you are set up to effectively tackle your business ideas. When someone comes up with a business idea and asks you, "Think people would buy this?" you can answer, "I'm not sure, but I know how to find out." Cue handing them a copy of this book to teach them how to do it.

To conclude, I wish you the best of success in the business ideas you want to pursue. I hope that through the Cold Call Karate process you find an idea that turns out to be a real winner.

So go forth, make those calls, become a successful entrepreneur, and make your dreams come true!

PS. If you liked this book, I'd love for you to go on Amazon.com and leave me a review. Any sort of feedback would be much appreciated. If you have any questions you can also email me at ryan@growanempire.com, I'm always happy to help. If you want to learn more about me, check out my blog Growanempire.com

CHAPTER 7:
Acknowledgements

Ryan Mulvihill

ACKNOWLEDGEMENTS

NO BOOK IS complete without acknowledging the long list of people that helped turn it into a reality.

My parents, Josie and Ed, for supporting my dreams to move abroad and live in Chiang Mai, Thailand. They have always encouraged me to pursue my crazy entrepreneurial ventures. I think they are still holding out hope for me to get a masters degree though. Sorry mom, ain't gonna happen.

My preliminary readers: Tommygun, Michael L, Luke, Milo, Camille, Annika, Shashley, Chuck, Keith, Patrick Hood, Dejan, Jibs, Arvin, Matthew, Lina, Noameo, RAVATRON 5000, Nickles Pickles, Jeffrey, Chris, Maxipad, Mathias, Bald Russian, Femi, Keven, Natalie, Sol, Booya, Michael Di, Michelle Di, Elaine, and of course my awesome little brother Stephen.

All my pre-readers and peers from The Foundation, thank you all for the amazing support!

I want to give Dane Maxwell and Andy Drish from The Foundation a big thank you for teaching me the basis of this process through their course. If you want to learn how to build a SaaS business with no idea and no money I recommend you check them out at Thefoundation.com

Nick Loper from Sidehustlenation.com. He created an amazing Udemy course on the process of creating an ebook and launching it. He opened my mind to promotion tactics I didn't even know about before.

Tim Ferris, author of *The Four Hour Workweek* can be credited for getting my mind thinking about starting my own business. Read *The Four Hour Work Week* if you haven't, it will change your life.

Sean Ogle, from Location180.com for inspiring me to make the leap to location independent entrepreneur and travel Asia.

Mike Cernovich from dangerandplay.com for giving me a winning mentality when it comes to chasing my dreams.

Victor Pride from boldanddetermined.com for teaching me discipline to pursue this project.

Robert Koch from 30daystox.com where reading about his experiments for building online assets really inspired me to learn as much as possible.

Chris Lambert for not editing and giving me edits and feedback on my book, not once but twice! Check out her beautiful art pieces here http://chrislambertfineart.com

Noam Lightstone from lightwayofthinking.com for giving me endless advice on how to do my ebook the right way. Check out his book, Mastery of the Mind, here

Matt Rott for editing this book. I didn't realize how bad my grammar was until he looked it over. If you are looking for a great editor you can inquire about his services here: mattrottediting@gmail.com

Pooya Tolideh for designing the cover of my book. His artistic genius is one of the reasons this book sold so well. Check out his other designs at PixelPooya.com

And of course you, my reader, for taking the time to read this book and put it into action. I wish you the best on your entrepreneurial ventures!

Printed in Great Britain
by Amazon